TEAMING
for
QUALITY IMPROVEMENT

A Process for Innovation and Consensus

Dr. H. David Shuster

PRENTICE HALL
Englewood Cliffs, New Jersey 07632

Library of Congress Cataloging-in-Publication Data

Shuster, H. David.
    Teaming for quality improvement : a process for innovation and
consensus / H. David Shuster.
        p.   cm.
    Bibliography: p.
    Includes index.
    ISBN 0-13-896739-3
    1. Work groups.   2. Quality circles.   I. Title.
HD66.S54 1990
658.4'036--dc19   88-33055
                                                            CIP

Editorial/production supervision and
    interior design: Cheryl Adelmann
Cover design: Wanda Lubelska
Manufacturing buyer: Mary Noonan

© 1990 by Prentice-Hall, Inc.
A Division of Simon & Schuster
Englewood Cliffs, New Jersey 07632

Printed in the United States of America
10 9 8 7 6 5 4 3 2 1

ISBN 0-13-896739-3

PRENTICE-HALL INTERNATIONAL (UK) LIMITED, *London*
PRENTICE-HALL OF AUSTRALIA PTY. LIMITED, *Sydney*
PRENTICE-HALL CANADA INC., *Toronto*
PRENTICE-HALL HISPANOAMERICANA, S.A., *Mexico*
PRENTICE-HALL OF INDIA PRIVATE LIMITED, *New Delhi*
PRENTICE-HALL OF JAPAN, INC., *Tokyo*
SIMON & SCHUSTER ASIA PTE. LTD., *Singapore*
EDITORA PRENTICE-HALL DO BRASIL, LTDA., *Rio de Janeiro*

*This work is dedicated
to my father . . . my anchor with the past,
and to my sons, Scott and Mark . . .
my windows to the future.*

CONTENTS

PREFACE

Seek the unpredictable . . .
Yearn for surprise

Teaming! Human empowerment through intellectual liberation. Individuals, working together, within formal procedures, encouraging an environment of free expression, innovation, and consensus, to decide an issue, solve a problem, or improve a condition. This book is about how such teams work. It takes you along on a **Teaming** journey and gives you the vicarious sense of being there.

Teaming is a part of most participative quality improvement processes suggested by respected experts. But there are relatively few published works that examine the detailed interdependent human behaviors shaping the enterprise. That is the focus of this book. We shall consider such questions as "how do I form a team . . . how do we start once we are seated around the table and ready to go . . . what should individual members do and not do . . . what techniques can we use to stimulate and exploit creativity, innovation, good will, and consensus . . . what happens when the process breaks down and chaos seems to rule . . . what rules and procedures must we follow and when can they be changed . . . what limitations and difficulties do teams usually experience . . . how is the process to be evaluated and decisions implemented . . . what happens if top management does not support us . . . and how do we overcome cynicism?"

Note that my emphasis is on "teaming," a verb, rather than "teams," a noun. Action, "doing," is the critical **Teaming** unit of analysis, not things, "being."

Teaming is an activity conducted to *actualize* central principles of quality improvement, that is, to operate and apply them. If principles are meant to directly influence behavior and performance, then mechanisms must be engineered to bring them to life. **Teaming** is one such mechanism.

There are numerous designs and models for conducting collective decision making. Many of them focus on problem solving. But problem solving is only one topic of interest to people. Things do not always go wrong, yet people still require meetings. Sometimes the intent is simply to examine what is happening or to imagine what could happen. At other times, interest is directed toward improving what is already functioning properly. Quality minded people do not accept the well-worn dictum "if it ain't broke, don't fix it." They would counter with "if it's broke, fix it . . . if it ain't broke, then improve it." Therefore, the Process for Innovation and Consensus (PIC) model that I suggest begins by looking at *symptoms* instead of *problems*. Problems are merely one possible subset of symptoms.

I have tried to link the PIC and its techniques to the general body of quality improvement theory. But my primary purpose is to describe and analyze the act of **Teaming** with sufficient insight and detail to give the reader enough direction to try it. This book should prove very useful to both inexperienced and experienced team participants as a guide to the **Teaming** rationale, form, structure, and procedure. Anyone who is even slightly interested in management, organizational behavior, productivity improvement, and quality improvement will find this work useful. It fits in academia and in industry.

My writing style is informal . . . very informal. First and second person references are as prevalent as third person references. This is not the stuff of mathematical models, charts, and formal organization charts. It is the stuff of individual human beings.

Chapter 1 introduces the idea of **Teaming** and offers a few hints about what **Teaming** *is* and what it *is not*. Belief and faith in the process are also discussed.

Chapter 2 juxtaposes five well known and authoritative definitions of quality and suggests that they emphasize a single theme presented from different perspectives. Debates concerning an appropriate definition appear to be neverending. I like to think that these few pages will shed some light on a different way of looking at the question. I offer my own definition of quality and show how it relates to the others. Finally, I suggest that they are all useful.

Next, I look at the difference between *indicators* and *measures* as devices for verifying performance and outcomes. At this point, I introduce the first of *Shuster's Laws*. These eight rules of **Teaming** are critical enough to be considered universal.

Chapter 3 is a short detour into the land of commitment. Everyone seems to believe that commitment is the most vital ingredient of quality improvement. But few people spend much time and energy dissecting it and observing it under a microscope. I offer a short analysis by arguing that, at root, commitment is an ethical decision that every individual must personally make. Then I suggest two definitions of commitment, one each from a negative and positive perspective. The discussion ends with a corollary to the oft-stated truth that quality management cannot be achieved without commitment. That corollary adds that it can begin without commitment. All that is needed is endorsement, commitment's weak, but far more familiar, sister.

Chapter 4 is an excursion into some characteristics of human behavior that are important to understand within the contexts of quality improvement in general and **Teaming** in particular. I look at adversarial and cooperative behavior styles, individual and collective interests, and the vast differences between manipulation and leadership. I also offer a definition for leadership that centers on individual character traits. The strengths of individual expression and collective consensus, so characteristic of **Teaming**, are explained in terms of eighteenth-century classical liberal principles of the free market economy. With respect to leadership, I argue (with Plato) that the true test of leadership is not in its origin in the one, few, or many, but rather in its beneficiaries. Do leaders serve themselves or their constituents? That is the key, in business organizations no less than in politics.

Chapter 5 gets to the heart of applications. The PIC model is fully described and illustrated. At first, my model looks a bit more complicated than necessary. But I have found that some models identify individual steps without clarifying the overall pattern and intent of the process. Therefore, I begin with a very general two-phase process, break each phase into two subordinate stages, and further subdivide each stage into a number of steps. The idea is to understand both the forest and the trees. Each step begins with a question. It ends with the answer, which implies another question/step/answer, and so on. The logic of the PIC is simple:

- ○ Identify a symptom
- ○ Determine the root causes
- ○ Target recommendations against those few root causes that account for the bulk of the symptom
- ○ Determine:
  - ○○ How to implement the recommendations
  - ○○ The possible consequences of the recommendations
  - ○○ The feasibility of the recommendations

None of this is particularly earth shattering or original. But, the PIC does offer some new twists and linkages of principle and practice to the discipline.

Chapter 6 is the center of the book. It is long. It is detailed. It adds to the literature by offering an examination of **Teaming** techniques that is full, detailed, and complete. Techniques are the thinking tools used to conduct the various PIC steps, very much like hammers and saws are the tools for conducting the various steps of carpentry. With the exception of Juran's discussions of Pareto analysis, these techniques (some familiar and some original) are dissected to a degree seldom found throughout current quality improvement literature. The chapter begins with an explanation of how the process (PIC) and the techniques interrelate. This is followed by nearly 80 pages of detailed analysis of each technique. Each technique discussion is divided into two sections, *features* and *procedures*. The features section presents the intent and characteristics of the technique. The procedures section contains a step-by-step outline of how to conduct the technique. Table 6-2 identifies which techniques are used in each specific PIC step.

Chapter 7 adds some color regarding the kinds of things that happen in a functioning team room. These are human beings behaving in the room and anything can happen. I talk about the role of the facilitator, a topic (along with commitment) worth another book. The chapter includes a list of different kinds of teams and how they can be coordinated to ensure universal participation of all personnel (Table 7-1 and Figure 7-1). It is important to understand that quality circles are only one of many kinds of teams and are, sometimes, the least preferred.

The second topic discussed in this last chapter introduces a behavioral systems model that offers a reason why **Teaming** works so well as a quality improvement mechanism. Derived from engineering control systems theory and social sciences systems analysis, the model suggests that any organization's best guarantee for survival, in a risky and uncertain competitive world, is the ability to positively adapt to stress. Positive adaptation means more than simply reacting to stress (passive adaptation). It refers to proacting in the face of threats to survival by turning their energy to favorable use. The mechanism for such adaptation is feedback, the ability to adjust behavior by sensing the results of previous behavior. **Teaming** actualizes such virtues and is, therefore, a superb mechanism for operationalizing quality improvement and enhancing corporate survival and growth.

Appendix I lists Shuster's eight laws of **Teaming.**

Appendix II is a detailed description and analysis of the systems adaptation model introduced in Chapter 7. I took it out of the mainstream of the book because the details will interest only some readers.

ACKNOWLEDGMENTS

How do I recognize so many people who, over so many years, have helped me to achieve this end? Forgetting anyone is unforgivable, but including everyone is unimaginable.

A number of my graduate and undergraduate professors influenced my life and thinking so much that they must, collectively, be mentioned. The same must be said for many colleagues and students who passed through my faculty years. My tenure with the RCA Service Company (now General Electric Government Services) introduced me to individuals who I must commend, again collectively, for their encouragement, wisdom, and insight.

However, certain people played a direct role in encouraging and advising me in the preparation of this book. Dr. Don Morgan, former head of the California Polytechnic Institute Industrial Engineering Department, introduced me to Prentice-Hall, read my manuscripts, offered sage advise, and, most of all, listened to me till, I am sure, his ears numbed. Joe Cipriano, the deputy director for Weapons and Combat Systems at the Naval Sea Systems Command (NAVSEA) in Washington, D.C., was on the leading edge of quality improvement in the government long before it became popular. Joe offered me opportunities that significantly contributed to my thinking on this topic.

The Naval Ship Weapon Systems Engineering Station (NSWSES) is one of about 20 NAVSEA field activities. I have been associated with NSWSES, located in Port Hueneme, California, as an engineering contractor for ten years. Certain people there have been constant friends and companions, acting as sources of inspiration and participating in **Teaming** activities whenever called upon. My worst fear is that some of their names will escape this statement of recognition. To those who undeservedly reside in that category, let me apologize now.

Billie Edwards, Gene West, Bob Berryman, Charlie Giacchi, Commander Ron Roundtree, Tom Rutkowshi, and Tommy Thompson, Wally Terry, and the technical director, Ted Rains, were some of the first people to step out in the new quality direction.

About two years ago, the government quality improvement process got started in earnest at NSWSES. Gene Fisher, the associate director for Weapon Systems, became the first executive to put **Teaming** to the test. Jay Eason and Mike Sauthoff were appointed by the technical director to develop and administer a Quality Programs Office to coordinate all station quality and productivity improvement efforts. They got it all rolling. Since then, a virtual parade of people has found the beat of the quality drummer. Captain Bob Jones, Dr. Ross Cohen, Tom Meyers, Mike DiVriend, Kathleen Durmier, Lloyd Vancil, Phil Anastasia, Jim Sebring, Al Signor, Marshall Scheaffer, and dozens of others have performed on instant action teams, extended action teams, and various other activities with energy, enthusiasm, selflessness, and inspiration.

Terry Williams, Joel Wells, and Warren Dietz of NAVSEA also contributed ideas influencing elements of this book. I must not forget Valerie Ashton of Prentice-Hall. Her faith in me, throughout this enterprise, is remembered. And I cannot forget Cheryl Adelmann. She never said no to a reasonable request concerning book production. To Lisa Christensen, my long suffering word processor, all I can do is thank you and join your glee at this end. Enjoy your vacation.

As for my patient and enduring family, there is little to say that might compensate for paper, books, and stationery objects strewn everywhere, 2:00 A.M. typing, blank stares, an inattentive mind, and the general eccentricities of a reasonably normal human being turned "writer."

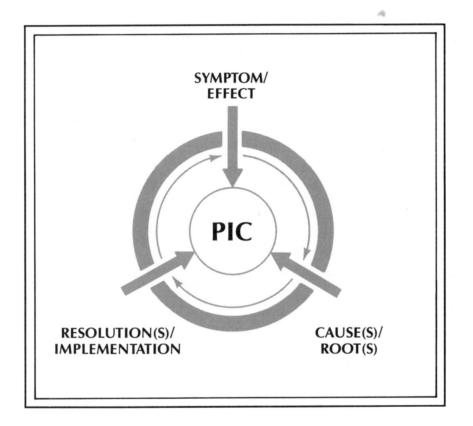

PART ONE

CONCEPTS
Thinking About It

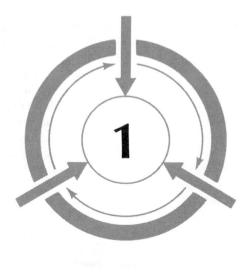

THE IDEA

A young lady approached me at the close of a one-day **Teaming** orientation session that I had just conducted for her organization. "Dr. Shuster," she exclaimed, "I have never met anyone as enthusiastic as you. And it's catching. After 15 years in this place, I didn't think it was possible to ever get excited about my job again." She flashed her eyes and exclaimed, "You're like an evangelist!" Realizing that she had struck true, I chuckled back that I would take that observation as a compliment. She assured me that it was.

If evangelism means believing in something true and spreading its good news, then color me evangelist. I believe in quality improvement as the single best way of achieving productivity improvement and as the single best guarantor of corporate survival, success, and leadership in uncertain, risky, complex, changing, often hostile, international competitive markets. I believe that innovation is a vital key to quality improvement. I believe that the ultimate source of innovation is the creative mind of each unique **individual** who populates an organization and that, therefore, every single human being in that corporate body is precious and must fully participate in the effort. I believe that people are creatures of deep professional integrity and that the surest way to inspire and mobilize the fruits of their moral honesty is to show, by word and deed, that their dignity is recognized and respected. I believe that one of the most electrifyingly powerful ways to mobilize the too often untapped energy locked in those minds is to join them into teams. Not any old kind of committee! I mean very specially organized collectives that exploit the latent creativity locked within each participant and then generate typically unheard of levels of consensus about issues otherwise deemed unresolvable. This very special small organization is centered around a group decision-making concept that I call a *Process for Innovation and Consensus* (PIC, pronounced "pick"). PIC is not entirely original, but there is much within it that is original. It borrows heavily from the social sciences, arts, control systems theory, moral philosophy, and many highly respected techniques that are generally familiar to quality improvement professionals. My purpose in this book is to guide you, the reader, through the quality **Teaming** "looking glass" into the world of PIC, to impart to you the vicarious experience of "being there." Understand . . . my mission is not merely to inform you, but to "touch" you, to excite your imagination and leave you wanting more.

This is not a book about "quality circles" or some such other specifically defined type of team. Most assuredly, circles (or any other kind of quality improvement team) can (and do) use variations of PIC-like processes. But they do not *have* to use them. I shall suggest a number of different organizational types of teams that can use PIC. Quality circles are certainly one of them. But only one! The universe of possible team types, I have found, is virtually limitless. Everytime I look around, someone has found a new organizational variation for bringing people together, and a whole new spectrum of opportunities emerges. These opportunities seem to share one set of phenomena in common, the reawakening of dormant hope. Year after year, I watch dulled eyes gleam anew, silent despair rekindle into heightened expectations, cynicism surrender to fresh idealism, narrow self-interest bow to reborn trust, and intimidation recede behind reenergized self-respect and courage. Small wonder that I never tire of the experience. Of course I am enthusiastic. Sure I believe!

One final note about the young lady who spoke to me after the one-day orientation session. Such meetings are usually the participants' first exposure to a PIC-type **Teaming** process. Therefore, I always arrange for a number of managers, executives, and/or peers to visit the session during the last half-hour to listen to the participants' answers to the question "Well, what did you think of it?" At the start of the day, I inform the group of this forthcoming event. I predict flat out that they will report this to be one of the very best professional experiences they have ever had. They usually chuckle at my presumption. I have come to subconsciously gauge the tone of that collective smirk as an unscientific estimate of the overall level of morale within their organization. With unerring repetition, the consensus of the groups is to answer the question by affirming my prediction. Certainly there are criticisms and doubts. And a few people do not feel comfortable with such a new process. But the candle is lit. The overall response is very positive. They typically rejoice at the absence of an intimidating atmosphere. Their most often expressed fear, by far, is that "good as this is . . . 'management' will probably give it some temporary lip service endorsement, and then ignore our suggestions; and we shall lose interest. It will become 'this year's fad'." The woman in my story was no exception. She happily agreed that the session was exactly as I had advertised, but expressed a hope for ultimate management acceptance that was dimmed by years of contrary experience. I told her that cultural changes are fraught with pitfalls and demand relentless determination, that is, commitment. She believed me when I said that organizations little different from her's have "turned it around." Her particular department is trying to do just that, with some patient success.

PIC works! It also evolves. No less than any survival-seeking entity, it must positively adapt (as discussed in Chapter 7 and Appendix II) to the changing currents of time and circumstance. It is subject, no less than its students and users, to the imperative of innovation. A process for innovation must, itself, innovate or wither in the winds blowing things that were . . . into things yet to be.

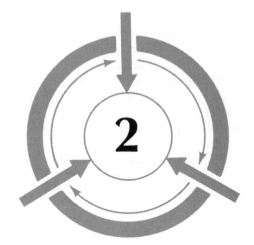

THE SINGULAR FACE
OF QUALITY

If you inquire what the people are like here, I must answer,
"the same as everywhere."

One must be something to be able to do something.

Just trust yourself, then you will know how to live.

Individuality of expression is the beginning and end of all art.

Johan Wolfgang von Goethe

There are probably as many definitions of the term quality as there are quality experts. So it should not be entirely surprising if some people express confusion about which definition is most accurate, complete, and acceptable. Actually, the differences between most generally respected definitions are not that great. They represent variations around a set of common themes and, as such, do not compete. They blend! Each expert defines quality according to his or her interest, viewpoint, and purpose. Students of quality improvement will enrich their understanding of the subject if they compare various authors' perspectives on the subject.

My perspective requires a definition of quality that focuses on the common elements unifying the variations. This is necessary because **Teaming** is a universal process, applicable to every quality improvement enterprise.

A UNIVERSAL PROCESS MUST TOUCH A UNIVERSAL THEME!

TYPICAL QUALITY DEFINITIONS

Typical definitions of quality emphasize one of three universal product or service development perspectives: process, outcomes, or consequences. Experts generally agree that every product or service is created through some performance *process*, that is, a sequence of events in which people use resources to convert some mixture of inputs into another mixture of outputs. One example is the process in which a fast-food retailer converts raw foods into a complete dinner, attractively packaged and ready to consume. The *outcomes* are the dinner, the dining environment, and convenience. They are the *outputs* of the process. The *consequences* involve the impact of the outcomes on both the immediate user and society at large. For instance, the convenience of drive-through-eat-on-the-road is a positive consequence of the packaged food outcome for travelers. A potential negative consequence for society at large is the pollution caused by the user throwing the empty food wrappers, cups and bags onto the side of the highway. In summary, performance processes create outcomes that have consequences.

Table 2-1 lists five representative and respected definitions of quality offered by Genichi Taguchi, J. M. Juran, Philip Crosby, Kaoru Ishikawa, and W. E. Deming. Taguchi and Juran focus on the impact that the *consequences* of the product/service have on customers and society after it transfers from the seller to the buyer. Crosby and Ishikawa concentrate on the inherent character of the product/service *outcomes* before it is so transferred. Deming emphasizes the performance *process* that creates and makes the product/service ready to be transferred to customers.

A moment's thought should make it clear that these definitions of quality are not divisive. Quite the contrary! They are mutually supportive, giving the reader enriching and varied insights around the common theme of excellence.

TABLE 2-1 Summary of Five Representative and Respected Definitions of the Term Quality

Author	Perspective	Quality Definition Summary
Taguchi	Consequences	The loss a product causes to society after being shipped, other than losses caused by intrinsic functions
Juran	Consequences	Fitness for use
Crosby	Outcomes	Conformance to requirements
Ishikawa	Outcomes	Nondispersion of quality characteristics[a]
Deming	Process	Process promising to result in products/services that can be sold to customers who will be ultimately satisfied[a]

[a]Not explicitly stated by the author, but derived from my interpretation of his total presentation.

Viewed upstream from either Juran's or Taguchi's *consequences* perspective, the positive or negative consequences of a product/service result from the character of the outcomes, which are themselves the result of the performance processes that created them (Figure 2-1). Deming looks the other way. He starts with the *process* and sees outcomes and consequences as downstream effects. Together, they sculpt a full and single face of quality, as seen from several vantage points. Their diversity of viewpoint emphasizes their unity of theme.

MY DEFINITION OF QUALITY

My ultimate purpose, stated earlier, is to find a definition of quality that meets the universal requirements of **Teaming**. Consequently, my definition should encompass the intent of all definitions, including the five cited above. Although they share the theme of excellence, that is too abstract a concept upon which to hang my emphasis. I need a common element that is tangible, concrete, and directly observable. That necessary linking element is *individual people*. People are the creatures who experience *consequences*. People are the parties by and for whom *outcome* requirements are established and product/service characteristics spawned. And people are the beings that "do" the performing (or controlling) in performance *processes*. People are also the central

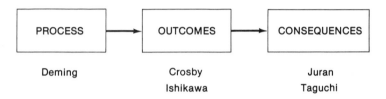

Figure 2-1 Five Authors' Perspectives on Quality

actors in **Teaming**. Therefore, my definition of quality must orbit around one or more characteristics of people.

A clue to what those characteristics might be is found in the total quality management literature written by such widely respected experts as the five authors identified in Table 2-1. Regardless of their differing definitional perspectives, they agree on the principle that to convert an organization from traditional management practices to total quality management practices requires fundamental changes in human attitudes and behavior, that is, cultural mutations. The idea is that, if such alterations occur, then traditional performance processes will yield to improved performance processes, with the added dividend of encouraging the search for even greater improvements . . . over and over again. This ensures better and better outcomes, which cause increasingly satisfactory consequences.

People's attitudes and behavior, then, are the linchpins of quality. And it is from this insight that my definition of quality emerges. Were my name added to Table 2-1, it would be properly located under Deming's. My entry under the perspective column would be *individuals*.

My definition of quality, entered under the quality definition summary column, would be:

THE RELENTLESS INDIVIDUAL PURSUIT
OF
CONTINUOUS PERFORMANCE IMPROVEMENT

Quality, viewed this way, is a dogged personal quest after perfection. My perspective is upstream of the others (Figure 2-2). From the individual human source comes all else. Looking downstream from my perspective, quality creates improved performance *processes* (Deming), better *outcomes* (Ishikawa and Crosby), and more satisfactory *consequences* (Juran and Taguchi). The definitions of the five included authors are not, then, examples of *quality itself*, but are, instead, examples of the *results of quality*, that is, the downstream effects of quality.

No wonder definition perspectives differ. Quality has limitless results. No wonder they are so unified. Quality is their single source.

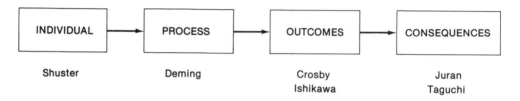

Figure 2-2 Six Authors' Perspectives on Quality

It takes a while to get used to the idea of quality as a human pursuit. Quality, traditionally understood as a process, outcome, or consequence, carries the implication of a thing, a noun. Now it implies an action, a verb. Remember, however, that it is tangible human beings (things) "doing" the acting.

Personally, I believe that all the cited quality definitions have substantial merit. Choose the most useful for a given purpose and let listeners know from which perspective you are thinking. A beautiful jewel is most appreciated when viewed across many facets.

QUALITY INDICATORS AND MEASURES

How would quality be measured within this context? Numerous ways! For instance, a long list of indexes are suggested by Deming's 14 points, Crosby's maturity grid, and many elements defined by the other cited authors. Examples include the number of company employees participating in specified quality improvement processes, specific behavioral illustrations of Deming's "constancy of purpose," numbers of unsolicited ideas captured and implemented as a correlate of his "driving out fear," examples of Crosby's "nonconformances to requirements," and so on. Add to these the generally familiar downstream measures enumerated by a vast body of existing literature, and a pool of verifiable quality tests exists to satisfy any standard.

A generally valid principle of measurement can be expressed as the first of what I shall call *Shuster's laws*, the rules of PIC **Teaming** that I consider to be universal and immutable.

Shuster's Law #1 states:

> YOU CAN MEASURE ANY HUMAN ACTION
> THAT YOU CAN OBSERVE.

Anything that can be sensed, therefore, can be measured and evaluated. It makes no difference if outcomes are products or services, tangible or intangible. Quality can be effectively defined. And it can be measured for effect.

Sometimes it is not necessary to measure reality in order to understand what is happening. Verification can be accomplished by simply identifying certain *indicators* of events and relationships. The basic difference between indicators and measures is *precision*. Indicators are imprecise. Measures are precise. Indicators are, therefore, less certain and objective vehicles of verification. For example, indicators that a person is sick might include sweating and clammy skin, flushed color in the face, coughing, listlessness, and a very warm forehead. Most people would treat these as signs of illness, but not as verification of flu or strep throat or some other malady. Precise verification would include taking certain measures, including taking the person's temperature, extracting blood and throat cultures, and the like. If the thermometer reads 101.5°, then we might properly say that illness is *measurably* verified. The results of the other tests would further pinpoint the character of the illness and, therefore, the appropriate treatment (solution) for a cure.

The trend from indicators to measures is therefore characterized by an increasing precision in representative signs of reality. Such signs are often called *measures*. They include:

○ *Nominal Measures*: Least precise indicators. They simply identify or name something. Examples include the numbers on a football player's uniform or the numbers identifying items on a written list of activities. The numbers bear no quantitative functional relationship to each other. For instance, the quarterback's number (12) and the tight end's number (68), if added, would equal the quantity 80. But that number would be meaningless with respect to conveying information about either the team, the individuals, or the progress of the game.

○ *Ordinal Measures*: Imprecise indicators. Numbers are used as substitutes for statements such as "more" or "less," or "small," "medium," and "large." Television movie critics usually rate films on "a scale of 1 to 10, ten being best." But there is no way precisely to define the distance in value between ratings of "1" and "2," or "6" and "9," anymore than there would be in defining the distance between "terrible," "very poor," and "poor," or "good" and "excellent." Statistically, for instance, there would be little value in calculating the arithmetic mean (average) of different critics' ordinal evaluations of a film. I would suggest the median as a more appropriate measure of central tendency in such cases. The reason is the lack of a standardized distance between numerical values. One could not, for instance, say that a rating of "9" equals the sum of "6" and "3," or "4" and "5."

○ *Interval Measures*: More precise crossover from indicators into measures. Distances between individual numbers are equivalent and known. For instance, the degrees of temperature registered on the thermometer used to gauge the person's illness are equivalently separated. The difference between 97° and 98° (1°) is the same as the difference between 101° and 102° and it is half the difference between 100° and 102°. What is missing in this Fahrenheit scale of temperature is a natural base against which to rate the absolute value of each reading. The Fahrenheit scale is referenced, by convention, to other temperature scales. In other words, the base is not rooted in some absolute standard found in nature.

○ *Ratio Measures*: Very precise. These are interval measures based on scales that are rooted in natural bases. An example is the temperature scale based on Celsius degrees. The base is absolute zero degrees, as found in nature. Therefore, the ratios of two different values, with respect to absolute zero, are mathematically meaningful and can be meaningfully compared with precision.

Too often, I believe, we insist on verifying quality in ratio terms, when something less certain will suffice, such as ordinal indicators. I would not, for instance, doubt the advice that the person showing signs of illness go home from work and get into bed. Taking an aspirin, drinking lots of juices, and calling a doctor would also, I believe, be reasonable suggestions. Immediate verification (measurement) could be enhanced (but not made certain) by taking his or her temperature. In such a case, we would be acting on the basis of indicators, not measures.

Actions must not *always* await measurement. They are often justified by indicators. Many quality improvement experts state that measurement is a critical element of the process. I would modify that statement to say that "verification is a critical element of the process, recognizing that degrees of verification are acceptable, from *indication* to *precise measurement*, as appropriate to each situation." This difference is more than semantic. It gets to the heart of evaluation, the knowledge of reality and justification for action.

The most significant measurement tool in the quality improvement arsenal is statistical process control (SPC). But I do not want to give the impression that this technique is an element within **Teaming**. Quite the contrary, SPC is an independent device that, along with **Teaming**, constitutes one of the central pillars supporting any total quality process. I commend you to Deming or any number of other experts for complete renderings of this topic.

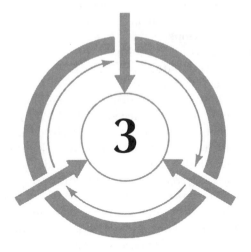

COMMITMENT:
MYTH AND REALITY

Attempts to internalize real quality improvement fail more times than we sometimes like to admit. More often than not the failure is due to a lack of *will*, rather than to a lack of *ability*. *Willingness* and *ability* are the necessary and sufficient conditions for success in any goal-directed enterprise. PIC **Teaming** improves ability and stimulates willingness. But it can be neither started nor sustained without some prior willingness. To fully internalize a quality culture into an organization, a very special kind of willingness is required. It is called commitment. *Commitment* is the vitamin that puts the "relentless" in the "individual *relentless* pursuit of continuous performance improvement." Commitment has a weak sister called endorsement. Both of these forms of willingness have a role to play in the quality enterprise. The ultimate role of commitment is, by far, the greater. Without it, a total quality process can be little more than a sweet dream. One sure sign that quality is totally embedded in the corporate culture is that "quality" is not one of several agenda items discussed during executive staff meetings. It is, rather, the umbrella under which all issues are discussed, that is, the foundation of the corporate plan and all subsidiary considerations.

Given the stress and emphasis that experts place on commitment as a crucial quality prerequisite, I am surprised at the relative lack of literature devoted to its investigation and analysis. This short chapter is a concession to that void. The dynamics of commitment and endorsement are important ingredients in the recipe for both successful PIC **Teaming** and total quality management. That fact, alone, justifies this discussion. But, even more significantly, I shall argue that the decision to seek quality is, fundamentally, an *ethical* choice. I shall also contend that the underlying guarantor of PIC **Teaming** success is the *integrity* of each individual group participant. A satisfactory understanding of commitment, therefore, will elude those who hunt its secrets only in the halls of systems analysis, decision models, statistics, and behavioral group theory. They must think philosophy.

I shall begin the discussion with a few assumptions, expressed as Shuster's Laws #2 and #3, and end the chapter with a definition of commitment and with a few unexpected optimistic conclusions.

INDIVIDUALS AS ACTORS

I suggest that the single most important, measurable unit of analysis in any performance process is each involved individual human being. Expressed as **Shuster's Law #2**, it states that:

> GROUPS AND PROCESSES DO NOT ACT . . .
> INDIVIDUAL PEOPLE DO!

Adapted from the work of political strategist Anthony Downs (1957), this imperative strikes to one central reason why PIC **Teaming** works so successfully. People often tell me that, in typical meetings, their individuality is submerged into a collective soup with everyone else. They do not participate . . . they attend. They are not asked . . . they are commanded and directed. They do not contribute . . . they obey. They do not ask "why" . . . they accept. They do not offer . . . they recognize caution and silence to be the better part of valor. What is worse, years of such experiences, taunted by the subconscious knowledge that this sterile intellectual environment is one's source of economic security, eventually intimidates people to reconcile themselves with what Henry Thoreau called "a life of quiet desperation." They simply do their job and "turn off."

PIC **Teaming** reverses all these dreadful conditions. Throughout the process, the individual is king, and cooperation between individuals evolves easily and naturally.

The gist of Shuster's Law #2 is that creative innovative ideas can only come from single minds; however, they may be kindled, stimulated, or encouraged by group associations. Consensus is also a summation of conclusions and attitudes framed in individual minds. Once people realize that their individuality is respected and accorded due dignity, they become eager to participate. Why? Because of **Shuster's Law #3**, which says:

PEOPLE ARE CREATURES OF INTEGRITY.

This is another root secret of PIC **Teaming** success. It means that people:

○ Approach responsibilities with honest positive motives
○ Have a natural desire to contribute to something worthwhile, that is larger than themselves
○ Value recognition from their peers
○ Treated with dignity . . . can be trusted

These assumptions are not based on the naive premise that there are no disruptive people in the world, that no one would systematically, and without provocation, take delight in undermining cooperative enterprises. But they are founded on the assertion that the chances of encountering even one such aberration in a typical working environment are low enough to dismiss. At worst, they are exceptions too rare to be declared as underlying principles of PIC **Teaming**.

Ask yourself if you go to work everyday intentionally bent toward the single-minded purpose of undermining the organization, destroying its ability to function, and ruining everything that your peers accomplish. Whenever I ask this question in a team training session, everyone laughs at the absurdity of such a suggestion. Therefore, I offer Shuster's Law #3 to the reader as a given. People are not diabolical!

It follows, then, that people should be trusted. Trust them with a vision and they will struggle to fulfill it. Let them think and they will create. Let them choose and they will decide. Let them act and they will perform. From out of cooperating individuals will come effective collective performance processes. Aggregated individual behaviors are the seedbed of the performance process-to-outcomes-to-consequences evolution. My definition of quality, given in Chapter 2, grew out of this premise.

AN ETHICAL PRESCRIPTION, A PATH TO COMMITMENT

Choosing to recognize another's inherent dignity and choosing to trust a peer's integrity are fundamentally *ethical* decisions; that is, the choices rest on a person's belief about what ultimate values are good, right, and proper. Out of such deeply rooted personal prescriptions about how one *should* or *should not* relate to other people grow the patterns of our interpersonal ties. The habits, lessons, and experiences of a lifetime are involved in such decisions and behavior. That is why it is so difficult to uproot the patterns regulating traditional organizational relationships, regardless of the formal benefits that change promises. But, as tough as change is to accomplish, such deeply implanted habitual roots must submit to alteration if real quality improvement is to be internalized within an established bureaucratic culture. And that is why quality must be a *relentless* pursuit. Anything less than a zealous chase is fruitless, agonizing, and fraught with peril. Dashing falsely raised hopes is far more damaging to employee morale and enterprise than is maintaining existing lowered expectations. Crushing anticipation damages the quality of work life more severely, universally, and permanently than maintaining a gloomy, but familiar, status quo.

Fortunately, however, life offers us choices. Cultural changes are possible. All that is needed is the *tenacious will* to achieve them. All that is needed is commitment . . . throughout the corporate population; but most especially at the top, in the executive suite. Commitment at the top is essential to achieving a total quality culture. But there is nothing particularly new or startling in this declaration. It is a commonly accepted truth among quality improvement students. However, it is an incomplete truth. Its essential corollary opens all sorts of new and exciting possibilities and offers hope to those who despair most about the potential for real change in their traditional work environment. I offer that corollary as **Shuster's Law #4:**

> THE QUALITY PROCESS DOES NOT HAVE TO *START*
> WITH COMMITMENT FROM THE TOP . . .
> . . . ENDORSEMENT IS ENOUGH!

Endorsement is known by many names and is recognized by everyone. It is "lip service," that is, verbal permission for *you* to "give it a try." The *top* tells the *bottom* that "it sounds good," and even suggests that "it might satisfy sponsor pressures to show evidence of an improving bottom line." That is not much to go on. But it is something. It is enough to start. Make no mistake; traveling on the uncharted quality "dirt path" of endorsement, without full backing from the chief rule makers, is a risky and rocky business. And you can be run off the road at any time. But it can be done! The trick is to seek, from out of the silent majority, those individuals who are willing and able to begin at the bottom to achieve some small success. Time and effort should not be wasted trying to convince the unconvincible. Facilitating the motivated will prove far more fruitful. And make no further mistake; such people *are* strewn throughout the organization, at every level of command . . . in the most surprising and unexpected corners. Tenacity, time, and demonstrated results are the catalysts that transform top management endorsement into commitment. Too many people have told me to forget a given organization because it is hopeless. But endorsement is a symptom of quality anemia, not corporate death. Would a physician refuse to treat a patient with a low blood count on the absurd premise that the person's anemia is, *a priori*, proof of death? What doctor would confine his or her practice to those individuals who are either healthy or totally unafraid to be treated? One's dread to admit illness is, itself, a symptom of malady, to be noted, understood, and accounted for by competent professional healers. The greatest challenge facing quality improvement practitioners (and their greatest opportunity) is to help those who lack willingness, rather than ability.

Make no mistake either about the fact that it is easier to trod the quality road with full *top-down* commitment. But that is like finding patients advanced, already, to the last stages of healing. By that time the quality process has usually been sufficiently internalized for the patient to conduct self-treatment.

The difficulty with *bottom-up* quality improvement strategies is that repeated positive results must occur relatively quickly. And the rug can be pulled out at any time. Such efforts require skill, diplomacy, political savvy, tenacity, patience, resilience, self-confidence, and a capacity to absorb abuse, disappointment, and even ostracism. It is, again . . . for each person . . . an ethical decision.

It is a tragic waste to write off organizations whose top managers are initially uncommitted to quality improvement. They are, after all, the most in need. And they are susceptible to the forces of selected pockets of commitment. They can . . . over time . . . be led to commitment.

COMMITMENT DEFINED

Commitment is a topic worth another book. For now, I shall simply define and characterize it from two polar perspectives, negative and positive. From the former viewpoint, *commitment* is:

OBSESSIVE INTOLERANCE FOR ANYTHING LESS THAN QUALITY,
THAT IS, FOR ANYTHING LESS THAN A RELENTLESS
PURSUIT OF CONTINUOUS PERFORMANCE IMPROVEMENT

Quality diminishes the instant someone says "it's o.k. the way it is . . . we can stop examining our performance; we already do quality work." Full commitment is manifested by a refusal to accept all the well-known excuses raised to restrain or delay the quality pursuit. Obstacles, to the committed practitioner, are merely barriers to demolish or sidestep on the determined journey to total quality management.

The positive side of *commitment* is:

FANATICAL TRUST IN THE INTEGRITY OF INDIVIDUALS AND A WILLINGNESS TO ASSUME THE BEST IN THEM

Such faith cuts through mountains of paper, spools of red tape, and multilayers of bureaucracy and reaches into the hearts of people . . . who respond in kind. Viewed from either perspective, the hallmark of a committed person is *passionate tenacity*. Moderation is no virtue and extremism is no vice when principle is at issue among the committed.

In Appendix II, I suggest a systems models to explain why quality-centered organizations succeed. The dynamics of commitment are crucial to that concept. So is passion. Too often we lose sight of the ideals that touch us in the rush to manipulate the systems that drive us. The adaptation model suggests that we succeed in enterprises by taking *positive*, as opposed to *passive*, actions to overcome stress and control our lives. We seize the day, rather than submit to it. Tenacious commitment, passionately held, is a vital prerequisite to such adaptive behavior. One must crave creative survival to achieve it.

In summary, quality is a single unifying force, a continuous, resolute, obsessive, tenacious, individual search for innovative performance perfection. It is driven by passionate commitment that is, at once, trusting of people and intolerant of denial. Commitment lends itself to "sweet reasonableness" only in questions of *means*, never of *purpose*. Yielding to endorsement at the start of the quality journey, commitment denies entry into the promised land without itself as the driver. Little wonder, then, that the stretch to quality, like the act of dieting, becomes for some, a tortuous lifelong excursion.

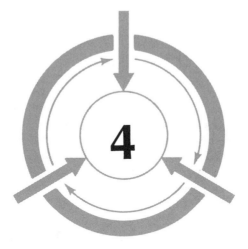

WHAT TEAMS ARE
AND WHAT THEY DO

Sir, I told those people . . . , "They fix the breakdown, not the blame."

Guidebook for Marines

Before we journey into the depths of PIC **Teaming**, a clear perception of what teams do, what they are, and what their limits are, should be clearly understood. Issues such as the balancing of competing interests, the foundations of assured success, participant selection criteria, the nature of creative thinking and consensus building, accommodation of rules, and the mood set by the overall **Teaming** environment must be addressed. Finally, the nature of leadership must be considered, including the question of how it is exercised in PIC **Teaming**. The reasons why PIC works become apparent from these principles.

BALANCING COMPETING INTERESTS

People are adversarial. They are also cooperative. While enjoying conflict in sports, business, and entertainment, they engage each other within accepted rules of competition. Some societies swing more to adversarial relationships, others to more deferential and cooperative styles. Whatever their tendencies, however, all groups must find mechanisms for balancing competing interests. Adversarial and cooperative styles are, in fact, two different methods for achieving that very end. As shown in Figure 4-1, adversarial people like to win, while their counterparts search to belong. The former want to compete, where the latter attempt coordination. But interests are the linchpin binding both efforts.

Consistent with **Shuster's Law #2**, only an individual can have an interest. An *interest* is that which serves an individual's purposes. Collective interests do not independently exist. They constitute some mixture of shared mutual individual interests. The character of that mixture determines the tightness of the unity binding the individuals together. Some collective interest associations are loose, unbinding, and tenuous. They are defined as *coalitions* in Figure 4-2. *Teams* are more tightly bound and unified. The more congruent and compatible a faction's stated collective interests are with respect to the personal interests of its individual constituents, the more it is a team and less a coalition. This in no way suggests that one form is better or worse than the other. Virtue or evil *in purpose* determines such things, not the means of their attainment.

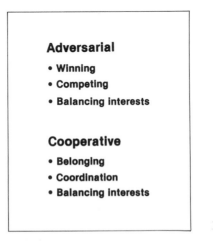

Adversarial

- Winning
- Competing
- Balancing interests

Cooperative

- Belonging
- Coordination
- Balancing interests

Figure 4-1 Behavior Styles

Individual

- **Satisfying**

  Optimum alternatives

  Inner directed

- **Satisficing**

  Acceptable alternatives

  Other directed

Collective

- **Coalitions**

  Common purpose

  Multiple separate independent interests

  Hidden independent agendas

- **Teams**

  Common purpose

  Coordinated independent interests

  Displayed common agenda

Figure 4-2 Individual and
Collective Interest

AN ECONOMIC INTERPRETATION OF TEAMING BEHAVIOR

In coalitions, individual members perceive the benefits of membership more in terms of unique private payoffs accruing to themselves (or to some subfaction), rather than to the group as a whole. In teams, individual members perceive benefits in the opposite light, as social payoffs shared in common with all group members. PIC **Teaming** inspires the best of both associations and diminishes their negative aspects. It promotes individuality in innovation and collectivity in consensus building. At all times, common interests and individual interests are expressed in terms of their mutual interdependence and joint compatibility.

One can reasonably ask why individual and collective interests should be assumed to be so compatible in the PIC **Teaming** environment when they might not be equally so in other settings. The reasons are that each PIC **Teaming** participant is free to express his or her personal concerns without fear of intimidation and that an atmosphere conducive to the free competition and consideration of all ideas is established. Individuals soon sense that their best personal choices become most obvious as more ideas are generated and considered and as the personal interests of their peers are encouraged coequally with their own.

One explanation of this phenomenon derives from the "invisible hand" concept of the eighteenth-century economist Adam Smith (1776). He sought to explain an apparently similar, but mysterious, compatibility between individual and collective interests in a capitalist market. He was specifically concerned about how a mutually agreed upon market price and quantity of output for any single product or service were achieved in a capitalist market, when it was abundantly clear that every single buyer and seller of that product or service was acting exclusively in his or her own self-interest. For instance, when individuals shop for a dozen apples, each tries to get the very best apples at the very lowest price. No one is particularly interested in the price that their neighbors pay. Similarly, each apple supplier tries to sell apples at the highest price he or she can get, with little or no regard for competitors' prosperity. Smith's answer, stated in the mysterious language of the *Invisible Hand*, was:

> Individuals . . . acting in their own self-interest are guided . . . as if by an "invisible hand . . ." to act in the collective interest.

Stripped of its apparent magic and mystical cloak, the principle is quite understandable to anyone who ever looked for a bargain or attended a sale. In any market (a mixture of buyers and sellers), each individual is motivated to participate (buy or sell) by self-interest, that is, to get the best possible personal deal. So the market is *driven* by self-interest. But it is *regulated* by competition, that is, by the fact that there are *many* buyers and sellers out there trying to get the best personal deal. Sellers know that they must offer better (or at least equal) prices than their competitors or risk losing customers. And buyers know that, if enough other buyers pay a certain price for the apples, they will be obliged to follow suit. Consequently, the price hunts for a level at which there are just enough buyers to clear the quantity offered by the sellers, that is, the price where the quantity demanded equals the quantity supplied. That price is usually called the *equilibrium price* or *market price* of the product or service being offered. If the actual price rises above the market price, then some buyers will leave the market and some sellers, seeing higher potential profits, will increase their stocks; that is, the quantity supplied will be greater than the quantity demanded. Once this *surplus* situation is recognized by both buyers and sellers, they will both tend to bid the price down toward equilibrium. If the price drops below equilibrium, then more buyers will be attracted into the market and sellers (seeing falling potential profits) will reduce their inventories. When this *shortage* condition is recognized by both buyers and sellers, they will both tend to bid the price up toward equilibrium. The amounts of these price fluctuations will diminish over time, and the price will settle at or near the equilibrium price determined by overall market conditions.

There is no joint planning in all this helter-skelter trading activity. Individuals do their self-interested thing, but the competition between them produces a consensual price. There are two necessary and sufficient conditions to make all this happen:

1. Individuals must be free to act in their self-interest.

2. An environment of free competition must be maintained.

The parallels between the economic free market and the PIC **Teaming** environment are more than superficial. Individual self-interest is the driver in both situations, along with a shared impulse toward an equilibrium consensus. In the economy, consensus is measured by an agreement on market prices and quantity of outputs. PIC **Teaming** participants derive agreements on issues of concern that best serve their individual and corporate needs. Prices and issues are merely two different currencies traded in the two respective environments. But both the market processes and PIC **Teaming** processes of individual innovation and collective consensus are quite the same.

LEADERSHIP

Everyone leads in a team! Which means, of course, that no *one* leads! Our typical reaction to such statements is to conclude that leadership, itself, must therefore be absent. That response is not only overly simplistic, it is also false. Leadership, to be present, must not be monolithic. It can be shared. And if it can be shared, there is no law of nature that says that it cannot be universally shared. The issue of whether it is most effective when residing in the hands of one, the few, or the many has been debated since the days of ancient Greece . . . and before. Plato and Aristotle asserted that political systems were good only if the *ruler* ruled in the public interest, that is, in the interests of the ruled (Sabine, 1962). They were bad if the *ruler* ruled in his or her own self-interest, that is, in the interest of the ruler. They defined a good *single* ruler as a *monarch* and his or her corrupt counterpart as a *tyrant*. A *few* ethical rulers are defined as *aristocrats*, while their villainous analogues are *oligarchs*. Many principled rulers are *democrats*, while their depraved opposites are *mobocrats*. Therefore, the test of proper leadership is not in its *numbers*, but rather in the directed *target* of beneficiaries.

The United States *Guidebook for Marines* (1984) makes a similar point by asserting that every Marine Corps private is a potential leader and that leadership qualities can be acquired by anyone willing and able to honestly examine themselves. The guidebook lists 14 character traits that define a good leader, the first of which is *integrity*. The unadorned core of integrity is honesty: "When you give your word, keep it. There are people depending on you . . ." (43-4). Again, the test of good leadership is its focus. Leaders are "squared away" only when their men are squared away, and each person's interest is best protected by the leader when everyone's interest is protected. This common logic, spanning several dozen centuries, is a centerpost of **Teaming** leadership, with the proviso that the source of leadership is diffused among all the participants.

Some people who occupy management positions do not lead. They manipulate. Like the authorities cited, I suggest that bad managers attempt to manipulate people, while good managers lead people. Leaders trust the integrity of their people and visibly demonstrate respect for each individual's dignity. Manipulators do not. Six behavior patterns characterize the different attitudes of manipulators and leaders, as illustrated in Figure 4-3. They include:

1. *Personal perception*: Manipulators view human beings as things, as mere devices to be used to suit whatever purposes are privately deemed appropriate. Manipulators might actually delude themselves into believing that they are serving the interests of those being manipulated, who simply "do not know better." Leaders respect their subordinates as peers who are the ultimate source of their own interest.

2. *Inspiration*: Manipulators leave people in alternate states of indifference, anger, despair, and/or frustration. Leaders uplift people with visions of what "they" can aspire to and achieve. They stimulate hope and high expectations.

3 *Mobilization*: Manipulators negatively drive people to act. The motivation for each individual is external and imposed more often than not. It is to escape punishment rather than to receive rewards. Leaders translate their inspiring visions into internal drives that self-mobilize people into actions consistent with those communicated uplifting visions.

To me, these three behavior patterns illustrate the essence of leadership. Therefore, I define *leadership* as:

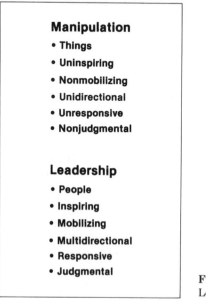

Manipulation
- **Things**
- **Uninspiring**
- **Nonmobilizing**
- **Unidirectional**
- **Unresponsive**
- **Nonjudgmental**

Leadership
- **People**
- **Inspiring**
- **Mobilizing**
- **Multidirectional**
- **Responsive**
- **Judgmental**

Figure 4-3   Manipulation Versus Leadership

THE ACT OF INSPIRING MOBILIZING VISIONS

Leaders allow people to glimpse their potential and show them pathways to attainment. The three remaining behavior patterns derive from this central premise. They include:

4. *Multiple directiveness*: Manipulators appreciate only one direction for the flow of influence: from themselves to the person (thing) being commanded. Only signs of obedience are permitted to flow back. Leaders expect, encourage, and accept the flow of influence in many directions, between all interested and participating individuals.

5. *Responsiveness*: Manipulators expect subordinates to simply react in a kind of knee-jerk fashion to directives. Underlings are not supposed to consider, analyze, ponder, or evaluate commands. They are to obey them . . . reasonable or not, feasible or otherwise, consequences aside. Leaders demand original thinking and "proaction" by their people. They appreciate ideas that can improve directives and stimulate positive considered responses.

6. *Judgment*: Manipulators act on the premise that their subordinates are agents of means, instead of ends. They reserve the right to determine appropriate ends and consider their peoples' role solely in terms of acting as means to attain those ends. Ethical judgments about the ends, therefore, must be left to the manipulator. It is not for subordinates to judge whether an end is good, right, or proper. Leaders assume that ethical judgments belong to everyone and recognize that every individual must balance his or her behavior on the fulcrum of personal values. They understand that ends might not justify means and that perverted means can distort legitimately intended ends. Their leadership instinct moves them to trust in the values of every subordinate as the best test of personal judgment.

Two cautions should be observed when considering these six manipulator/leader behavior patterns:

1. The patterns are oversimplified extremes. People are seldom, if ever, one or the other. Each of us demonstrates some mixture of these character traits. But, as extreme poles, they provide explicit standards against which each of us can evaluate our leadership abilities. And they provide goals toward which willing individuals can strive to become better leaders.

2. Manipulators are not devils and leaders are not saints. They are us! Leadership is a skill like any other craft. Our latent talents for it vary, just as they do for becoming champion track stars. But, whatever our natural endowments might be, we can all train ourselves to attain (and even

stretch) those limits. Teaming amplifies individual leadership capabilities by joining them, symbiotically, with those of our fellow participants so that the total group leadership is more than the sum of individual faculties.

It is now time to enter the world of PIC **Teaming**. The next three chapters walk us through the journey. Chapter 5 focuses on the PIC concept and outlines the phases, stages, and steps of the process. Chapter 6 introduces explicit, structured, thought-provoking techniques used to conduct the process. These tools of the trade are the equivalent to instructions for using hammers, saws, screwdrivers and chisels in the craft (process) of carpentry. Chapter 7 takes us into actual PIC **Teaming** rooms and allows us to watch and vicariously participate in the enterprise. Short of actually being there, this is about as close as your imagination can approach to the "sense" of it all.

PART TWO

APPLICATIONS:
Doing It

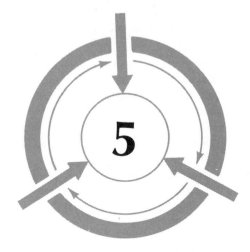

THE PIC CONCEPT

Do you wish to roam farther and farther?
See! The good lies so near.
Only learn to seize good fortune.
For good fortune's always here.

Johann Wolfgang von Goethe

One of the most prevalent misconceptions about quality teams is that they are, fundamentally, problem-solving agents. That idea severely restricts the universe of teams and violates one of the central tenets of quality improvement stressed by experts such as Deming, Juran, and Crosby. This theme states that the real breakthroughs in performance come after the severe, lingering, and chronic problems in an organization have been eliminated and totally new questions are asked about fundamentally new ways of doing things. A giant cultural hurdle is crossed when the idea of innovation is internalized in the minds, hearts, and habits of more and more people. Recall that my definition of quality (p. 10) zeroed in on this critical core. Teams, therefore, must be viewed as agents of innovation and consensus. That is their reason for being. The never ending journey toward the ever receding horizon of "something better" is traveled on the **Teaming** vehicle.

Therefore, the universe of issues studied by teams is virtually unlimited. Some issues might concern correcting things that are wrong (problems). Others might involve preventing future problems. Still others might turn us toward doing better what we already do well or doing what we have never done before. Consequently, from this point forward, think of PIC **Teaming** as a process for considering issues, within a virtually limitless scope.

PHASES, STAGES, AND STEPS

Countless books and essays have been written about problem solving, effective meeting principles, and group dynamics. Numerous how-to guides about quality circles have also been published. I have no intention of reinventing those wheels. Instead, I shall borrow, twist, and adapt portions of existing ideas, salt them with a few original thoughts, and present them in new dress . . . to advance the frontiers of participative management. My immediate purpose is to suggest a common vocabulary through which we can jointly build the PIC and understand its dynamics.

I suggest that the investigation of any issue is conducted in the following three *phases*:

1. Diagnosis
2. Prescription
3. Action

Diagnosis is the phase in which the issue is defined and its underlying causes identified and prioritized. *Prescription* is the phase during which it is determined what *should* be done to resolve the causes of the issue. The *action* phase involves executing and evaluation the resolution(s). The PIC includes only phases 1 and 2. Phase 3 is post-PIC. My experience suggests that the team members best suited to conduct the first two phases are not necessarily those most appropriate to perform the third phase. And, although many of the techniques used during the earlier phases can be used during the last phase, execution differs enough from analysis to warrant their separate consideration.

Each phase is conducted in two or more stages that are themselves divided into very specific tangible steps. The phase/stage relationships are illustrated in Table 5-1.

The *Symptom Selection Stage* (1A) is designed to define a broad issue in terms of one specific symptom selected from a ranking of suggested alternatives. Every issue can be defined (in whole or in part) in terms of some existing condition or symptom. A *symptom* is an observed, perceived, or imagined condition or state of things or events. For instance, a stomach ache is the symptom of a problem. It might be observed visually (swelling), by touch (heat), or by any of our five senses. It is either perceived or imagined by its victim. The symptom of an innovation-directed issue might originate, for example, in a shared perception that an existing customer service process, although satisfactory, could be significantly improved if customers' expectations and intentions were better understood, thereby increasing potential market share. During stage 1A, that general feeling might be refined into a specific symptom statement, such as "Our knowledge of customers' inclination to repurchase our product is uncertain."

We shall consider fully, in Chapter 6, that the symptom statement must be phrased in terms that imply no direct, tangible resolution. The reason is that human beings tend to jump to conclusions by assuming that they know the causes of a symptom immediately after becoming aware of the condition. Aside from the fact that this impatience might lead us to the wrong resolution, it prevents us from probing more deeply into causation and, thereby, opening our minds to unimagined and innovative insights, alternatives, and opportunities. Both of the example symptoms stated above meet this "no-implied-solution" criterion. The symptom statement, "I have a stomach ache," implies no direct, tangible solution. Imagine, for instance, your reaction if the doctor unhesitatingly replied to your complaint with the proclamation, "I am scheduling you for immediate surgery." The very absurdity of the response makes the point. What you properly expect from the physician is an examination. You want him or her to determine the cause(s) of your affliction and *treat (resolve) the cause(s), not the symptom.*

The *Cause(s) Identification/Prioritization Stage* (1B), therefore, begins with a speculative search for all the potential causes of the selected symptom.

TABLE 5-1   Issue Investigation Phases and Stages

Process	Phase	Stage
PIC	1. Diagnosis	A. Symptom Selection
		B. Cause(s) Identification/Prioritization
	2. Prescription	A. Resolution(s) Selection
		B. Implementation Planning
Post-PIC	3. Action	A. Execution
		B. Evaluation
		C. Adjustment

It ends with verified evidence about which few of the suggested potential causes contribute most to the symptom. At this point, both stage 1B and the diagnosis phase (Phase 1) end. We know at the time the symptom, and we know its primary contributing causes.

The next obvious question is "What *should* we do about it?" This prescriptive question leads us directly into Phase 2, Stage A, *Resolution(s) Selection*. During stage 2A, potential solutions are defined, means to their accomplishment are considered, their potential consequences (positive and negative) are analyzed, and refinements are added to accommodate feasibility and consequences considerations.

Stage 2B, *Implementation Planning*, follows directly and logically from stage 1B. Once the nature and implications of resolutions are understood, the next logical stage is to determine the mechanics, logistics, funding, scheduling, and measurement tools required to execute and evaluate the resolution(s). Hard data must be obtained to predict with some precision the expected cost/benefit outcomes of the projected resolutions. This stage is a process of translating resolution concepts into a concrete *plan* of action.

At this point, all that remains is to take action on the implementation plan. Phase 2 is complete, thereby terminating the PIC **Teaming** effort with respect to the selected symptom. Phase 3, *Action*, may be conducted by the same team members, a totally new team, or any desired mix of people. The three stages included within the third phase are designed to initiate, conduct, complete, and assess the results of the implementation plan. The final stage is to adjust operations in accordance with the results of the total process and, perhaps, begin again with another symptom related to the same issue. By this time, everyone's perspective on the issue will be substantially different than it was when it all started. New horizons, earlier unknown, will open new windows of opportunity and suggest alternatives only now becoming evident. From this rising yeast, new heights of understanding are reached.

Figure 5-1 outlines the PIC **Teaming** phases and stages. Note that resolution(s) are targeted only to those few critical causes that have been *verified* as contributing to the bulk of the symptom. It makes little sense to expend energy and resources on trivial causes, those that contribute insignificantly to the symptom. The overall PIC is then very simple in design. Isolate a condition of interest, define it as a symptom, verify its critical causes, specify reasonable, feasible resolutions, define expected costs/benefits and plan implementation of the resolutions. Remember that symptoms must be stated in terms that imply no direct tangible solution(s) to prevent the frequent human tendency to leap to wrong, unwarranted, or limited resolutions. Symptoms are to be viewed merely as the *effect* of one or more causes, which must be identified, ranked, and verified in terms of their degree of contribution to the effect. Solutions are targeted onto those few verified critical causes that, when treated, will resolve the symptom.

That is PIC . . . in outline. But, before we can move on to the tools and

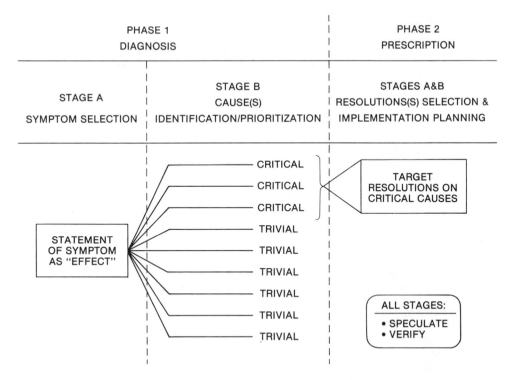

Figure 5-1   Process for Innovation and Consensus (PIC)

exercise of PIC **Teaming**, it is necessary to review the process again in terms of the specific steps into which each of its stages is further subdivided. These steps define the tangible actions comprising the phases and stages. Table 5-2 illustrates this subdivision. Specific steps are identified with three-character alphanumeric codes; for example, Step 2B1 is Phase 2 (Prescription), Stage B (Implementation Planning), Step 1 (Scheduling/Resources Speculation). The purpose of dividing and subdividing the PIC is to prevent people from forgetting the forest during their trek through the trees. Team members too often and too easily lose sight of the overall investigation process as they get entrenched in specific techniques and steps. It is a perfectly natural trap to fall into, and it is worth the up-front expenditure of time and thought to be warned of this pitfall. One of the **Teaming** facilitator's most important tasks is to prevent such tunnel vision from occurring.

At this point we understand the overall purpose and logical flow of the PIC in terms of its most general phases and semigeneral stages. The *steps* are merely those specific activities that must be conducted in order to proceed through the **PIC** journey and accomplish its purpose. Table 5-2 should be referenced periodically to keep a full perspective on the process. It can also be used to reorient those individuals who have temporarily lost their way.

TABLE 5-2   PIC Phases, Stages, and Steps

Phase	Stage	Step
1. Diagnosis	A. Symptom Selection	1. Symptom Speculation
		2. Symptom Verification
		3. Symptom Specification
	B. Cause(s) Identification/ Prioritization	1. Causes and Roots (C&R) Speculation
		2. C&R Verification
		3. C&R Prioritization
2. Prescription	A. Resolution(s) Selection	1. Solution(s) Speculation
		2. Consequences Speculation
		3. Solution(s) Refinement
	B. Implementation Planning	1. Scheduling/Resources Speculation
		2. Feasibility Verification
		3. Action Item Speculation
		4. Presentation

A few critical insights are gained by examining the steps in some detail. Note, for instance, that many of the steps involve *speculation*, the act of intellectual inquiry without need or recourse to demonstration, proof, or verification. Speculation is the key opening the door to free imagination, creative insight, new perspectives, originality, expanded vision, and altered horizons. Speculation is the mechanics of innovation. Therefore, it makes sense to speculate in every stage of the PIC.

Eventually, however, speculations must be ranked in terms of their usefulness in accomplishing our teaming purpose; that is, they must be demonstrated as being operational, measurable, applicable, and real. This is the purpose of the several PIC *verification* steps. For instance, the physician might speculate that one potential cause of a stomach ache is an ulcer. Another speculative cause could be gas, or appendicitis, or food poisoning, or whatever. Eventually, however, we shall expect *tests* to be taken, that is, empirical studies of temperature, pain, blood count, blood pressure, and other required measures that will verify which, if any, of the speculated causes is (are) the "real" cause(s).

The PIC, therefore, is a logically connected sequence of steps alternating between *speculation* and *verification*, with a sprinkling of prioritizations, refinements, and presentations inserted as catalysts in key spots. Clearly, innovation is central and evident throughout the process.

Consensus is less evident in this outline. Basically, it occurs at the end of each step, because what team members must agree on is that the step they are conducting is complete and it is, therefore, time to move on to the next step. Therefore, consensus is implied in the very act of progressing through the PIC steps.

"But . . . ," you might ask, ". . . how do you know when one step is finished and that it is time to move on to the next step? What criteria does one use to come to such a conclusion?" I hoped you might ask that question. The answer is that each step of each stage begins with a question that reflects the logical flow of the **PIC**. Each step ends when its initiating question has been satisfactorily answered . . . by consensus of the team members. And the rule of progression states that "when one step ends (by consensus), then the next step's question is automatically asked, thereby initiating that next step." The PIC ends when Stage 2B4 ends, that is, with consensus that its initiating question has been satisfactorily answered.

Table 5-3 is an expanded version of Table 5-2. Each step's initiating question is inserted between the Stage and Step columns. Take time, now, to carefully study the table. Read each step-initiating question in order of occurrence, keeping in mind its context within its stage and phase. Everything that follows is predicated on this logic. The fundamentals of the PIC are condensed into this single sheet and, like Table 5-2, it should be referenced as questions arise in forthcoming chapters. A hard-copy, pocket-sized, reproduction of Table 5-3 is included for your convenience. The asterisks (*) inserted at the ends of Steps 1A3 and 2A3 (far right) indicate points at which some teams choose to confer with their sponsors. The first conference, following step 1A3, is convened to discuss the question of whether the chosen specific symptom taps the broad issue of interest presented by the sponsor. This kind of review is not necessary. Many conditions determine the need for this particular review, and each team and sponsor group must set such rules for themselves. Whether the rules state that the sponsor has veto power over the specific symptom statement or that he or she has only the courtesy privilege of review is strictly up to those conducting the effort.

The conference at the end of the Resolution(s) Selection Stage (2A3) is also voluntary, but I personally suggest that it be conducted. As the initiating questions in Stage 2A indicate, the recommendations are pure speculations at the time. Their potential consequences have been thought about and ways to implement them have been considered, but they have not yet been verified. At such a moment, sponsors can contribute a great deal of insight and knowledge to the team. Sponsors might see potential consequences, for instance, that team members missed . . . or would have no way of knowing. Another major consequence of these meetings is the almost universal gain in admiration that sponsors acquire by observing the care and quality of the team's detailed analysis, innovative recommendations, and level of consensus. Ultimately, I have observed that team members also feel better about entering the implementation stage armed with the insights and support of sponsors regarding the solutions to be implemented. At such a time, the sponsor can also be useful as an agent for opening specifically defined doors, lining often reluctant bureaucratic corridors.

There is no formula for calculating how long is takes to conduct a specific PIC. It depends on many factors, including the character and qualifications of the members, the "grandness" and size of the issue of interest, timing, and

TABLE 5-3 PIC Teaming Phases, Stages, and Steps

Phase	Stage	Question	Step

1. D I A G N O S I S
 	
PIC
	A. Symptom selection	1. What is the observed or imagined condition (the symptom)?
		2. a. What empirical data are required to measure the speculated symptom?
		  b. Are required data available?
		  c. Do the data verify the speculated symptom, as stated?
		3. Is the validated symptom stated as an *effect*?
			1. Symptom speculation
			2. Symptom verification
			
			3. Symptom specification*

	B. Cause(s) identification/ prioritization	1. What are the potential causes and roots (C&R) of the specified symptom (the effect)?
		2. a. What empirical data are required to measure the relative contribution of each C&R to the specified symptom?
		  b. Are required data available?
		  c. Do the data verify each speculated C&R, as stated?
		  d. Can the verified C&Rs be ranked in terms of their relative contribution to the specified symptom?
		3. Which C&R's are *critical* and which are *trivial*, in terms of their ranked contributions to the specified symptom?
			1. C&R speculation
			2. C&R verification
			
			3. C&R prioritization

2. PRESCRIPTION	A. Resolution(s) selection	1. a. What are the most preferred potential resolutions to be targeted against the critical C&Rs? b. How can selected potential resolutions be accomplished? 2. What are the potential positive and negative consequences of the most preferred potential resolutions? 3. How can each preferred resolution be refined or improved?	1. Resolutions speculation 2. Consequences speculation 3. Resolutions refinement*
	B. Implementation planning	1. What are the predicted major milestones, who does it, who approves, and how is it funded? 2. What are the expected costs/benefits and are they feasible? 3. What specific action items are required to accomplish resolutions implementation? 4. How and to whom should these findings be presented?	1. Scheduling/resources speculation 2. Feasibility verification 3. Action item speculation 4. Presentation
		PIC TERMINATION	
3. ACTION	A. Execution	1. Are all required resources available and ready? 2. Is the plan initiated and operating?	1. Readiness confirmation 2. Accomplishment/monitoring
	B. Evaluation	1. What are the results?	1. Assessment
POST PIC	C. Adjustment	1. Is change or revision necessary?	1. Adjustment/confirmation

availability of required data. The size of the team is also important. I recommend teams composed of between eight and twelve members. The chemistry of participation seems to work best within that range. The group is small enough to remain personal and yet large enough to allow each person to build on a sufficient number of ideas for symbiotic innovation and consensus to occur.

One final caution. Teams require facilitators . . . unless most of the participants have extensive experience and have acquired knowledge of the process. In that event, a team leader can be appointed from out of the participants. This person does not take over or "rule" the proceedings. He or she merely carries out the normal member's role, but also acts as the "keeper of the process," helping to ensure that it is followed. Remember that PIC **Teaming** is a learned skill, and a proper investment in professional facilitator assistance is not only desirable, but absolutely necessary, for those early successes that motivate continued effort in the face of typical personal and bureaucratic obstacles.

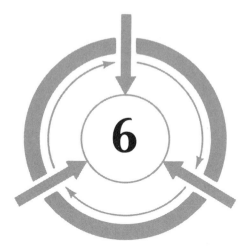

PIC TECHNIQUES:
TOOLS OF THE TRADE

It is sweet to let the mind unbend on occasion.

Horace

Love of bustle is not industry.
The best ideas are common property.

Lucius Annaeus Seneca

Criticism comes easier than craftsmanship.

Zeuxis

Give me where to stand, and I will move the earth.

Archimedes

Consider the little mouse, how sagacious an animal it is which never entrusts its life to one hole only.

Titus Maccius Plautus

Now, let it start. . . .

Shakespeare
Julius Caesar

PROCESS AND TECHNIQUES

Teaming is not easy. Neither is it a panacea. Participants typically report a sense of mental exhaustion at the end of sessions. But it is a sweet infirmity accompanied by the exhilaration of victory, the elation of real accomplishment, and a confirmation of one's capacity to overcome and achieve. The secret to all this is almost too simple to believe . . . in principle. The tough part is making it work . . . in practice.

Technique is the secret to making the PIC work in practice, that is, properly using the tools of the trade. The *trade* is the PIC. Techniques are the *tools*. Techniques are rigorously defined, logically related actions conducted to perform the PIC steps. Hammers, screwdrivers, and saws, by analogy, are the tools of the carpentry trade, including, of course, appropriate rules for their use.

There is a tendency for PIC newcomers to confuse the process (PIC) with techniques (tools). This is perfectly natural, but potentially frustrating. To be forewarned can help you to be forearmed. A few words now can prevent confusion later. This chapter is devoted to defining and explaining techniques.

Some team members who become confused between process and techniques compensate (usually unconsciously) by overritualizing technique performance. They tend to blindly and arbitrarily chant the rules, insisting that peers march more to the letter of the law, rather than to its spirit. Remember that innovation and consensus are the desired outcomes of the process. Techniques are tools that are justified only to the extent that their use serves the accomplishment of those process ends. Techniques are *means* to achieve ends. To raise the techniques, themselves, to the status of *ends* is equivalent to the carpenter treating the hammer, rather than the house, as the desired end. There are few dilemmas that can disorient and unmotivate a team more quickly than this particular situation.

To prevent such an occurrence, I offer a principle, often recited in words, but forgotten in application, and vital enough to be engraved as **Shuster's Law #5**:

TECHNIQUES SERVE THE PROCESS . . .
THE PROCESS DOES *NOT* SERVE THE TECHNIQUES.

Dismay and frustration await those who forget this dictum. Sad (and unnecessary) histories, recording the demise of quality circles and other teaming efforts, abound with wreckages run aground on this concealed shoal. Consider, again by analogy, the frustrated carpenter who fails to finish constructing a house because his hammer breaks. Connecting various boards of lumber is crucial to the construction process, and there are many tools available for accomplishing that end.

Ritual must not supplant meaning!

FAILURE AND FEAR

A sure sign that team members are forgetting the fifth law is a growing aura of frustration insidiously encircling the room, ultimately manifesting itself in a collective failure to proceed effectively through the PIC phases, stages, and steps. An alert facilitator senses it first in body language, blank stares, and assumptions implied by individual comments. Eventually, the drift becomes quite explicit. A typical cry expressing such advanced "gridlock" is something like "the process isn't working," or "see, it's failing."

Recall, however, that a process cannot fail! Techniques cannot fail! Only *people* can fail! Do not misinterpret this difference as a matter of mere semantics. It is quite fundamental. Remember **Shuster's Law #2**? Remember that processes are *concepts*, that is, structured ideas; that they do not "biologically live" . . . and breathe . . . and act? In this same sense, techniques are also ideas, expressed as precisely defined rules for action. But techniques cannot, themselves, *do* the acting. Only *people* can act! Obviously, then, only *people* can fail!

Remember, in **Teaming** neither the process nor the techniques *ever* fail. Individuals fail, sometimes singly, sometimes collectively, but always as individual people.

Why is this distinction so important? There are three reasons:

1. If people can fail, then people can fix.
2. The keys to fixing are contained in the process and the techniques.
3. There is nothing wrong with failure; failure is worthwhile and valuable.

Let us examine these three reasons in reverse order. First, what is so wrong with failure? Should good ends be abandoned for risk of failed means? Does the ten-month infant, learning to walk, fail by falling on his or her ample bottom in the attempt? Of course not! People learn techniques by trying . . . failing . . . and trying again. Ultimate success in completing the process comes from trying the techniques. This operating principle is contained in **Shuster's Law #6**:

FAILURE IS FINE . . .
FEAR OF FAILURE IS NOT!

Remember Deming's eighth point (within his famous 14 points of quality management): "Drive out *fear*" (1980). Sage advise! He did not say, "Drive out *failure*." Failure teaches! Fear destroys! Sophocles said it well: "To him who is in fear, everything rustles." Self-esteem and worthy enterprises drive out fear of failure or at least control its effects. This lesson is learned well in the "doing."

Reminding team members of these truths and guiding them to act in their accordance are crucial duties of facilitators. As in all things, prevention is better than cure. Skilled facilitators read moods and stop disfunctional things before they start.

As for reversing failures, as you read through this (and the next) chapter and imagine yourself acting a member's role, hold fast to the doctrine expressed in **Shuster's Law #7**:

THE PROCESS WILL SET YOU FREE!

This law's message is deceptively simple. When *you* are failing to conduct the PIC effectively, look to proven fundamentals for a remedy, that is, to the explicit rules of the process and its techniques. Your failure is in forgetting and/or abusing those guidelines. The remedy, therefore, is to remember and/or properly use them. Go back to them! It all comes with *practice*. Both the PIC and the techniques are user friendly. Practice soon *approaches* perfection. All that you have to do is be willing to:

○ Recognize failures
○ Admit them
○ Do something about them
○ Return to the process

Given such willingness, remedies come with relative ease.

Delightfully, appropriate remedial action always works and for logical reasons. Consider for a moment that, if only you and your peers can act and only you and your peers can fail, then it follows that only you and your peers can succeed. It is in your hands. Granting my overly simplistic reasoning, this fact holds quite true within the context of any given operating team. Shakespeare expressed the idea quite eloquently in the tragedy of *Julius Caesar*: "The fault, dear Brutus, lies not in our stars, but in ourselves, that we are underlings."

TECHNIQUES MENU

Everytime that I think I have an exhaustive menu of techniques, something new crops up. Sources are bottomless. A few of the included ideas are original; others come from literature, media, or someone else. My currently most used techniques are discussed in this chapter. Almost everyone will have heard of or used one or more of them, perhaps with variations of title or procedure. That is good. Avoid treating them as absolutes. Be creative. If you can substitute, add, or enhance the list, do so. I certainly expect to add to the list. However, do not make the mistake of being frivolous or sloppy with the use of any technique once it is selected. The rules of application are not arbitrarily defined. They are established with reason, wise or unwise, but with reason nonetheless. I shall endeavor to satisfactorily explain each rule for each technique. Do not violate those rules until you have exercised them enough to fully understand their intent, use, and *limits*. Freedom of choice is no excuse for arbitrary license. Remember that:

○ Your **Teaming** peers are also trying to comprehend the process and techniques, and a common language is crucial for effective communications and mutual understanding.
○ The techniques are not designed to be fully independent. The rules for each are derived with the others in mind. They are mutually interdependent. Consequently, when the rules of one technique are changed, its partner techniques can be affected, thereby influencing process phases, stages, and steps in unpredictable ways.

Therefore, although nothing is sacred . . . everything deserves sufficient respect to be changed only with reasonable care, insight, and sensitivity to potential consequences. Table 6-1 outlines and numbers PIC techniques. Review the entries to become familiar with the technique names and subelements before proceeding through the chapter.

TABLE 6-1 PIC Techniques

1 Divergence/Convergence (D/C)
  1.1 Divergence
      1.1.1 Nominal Group Technique (NGT)
      1.1.2 Brainstorming
          1.1.2.1 Random
          1.1.2.2 Structured
  1.2 Convergence
      1.2.1 Numbering
      1.2.2 Clarifying
      1.2.3 CDAM
          1.2.3.1 Combining
          1.2.3.2 Deleting
          1.2.3.3 Adding
          1.2.3.4 Modifying
      1.2.4 Lobbying
      1.2.5 Voting
          1.2.5.1 Multivoting
          1.2.5.2 Nominal Group Technique (NGT)
          1.2.5.3 Discrete Summation
2 Stream Analysis
3 Cause/Effect (C/E) Diagramming (Fishbone/Ishikawa)
  3.1 Factors Type
  3.2 Process Type
      3.2.1 Block
      3.2.2 Flow
4 Why–Because Pursuit
5 Process Internalization
  5.1 Informal Process Internalization
  5.2 Formal Process Internalization
6 Data/Information Accumulation
  6.1 Information and Data
  6.2 Pareto Presentation
7 How–By Pursuit
8 Force Field Analysis
9 Psychic Irrelevancy

COGNITIVE AND AFFECTIVE TECHNIQUES

Innovation requires the unrestrained use of all our creative juices. Sometimes ideas arrive as conclusions tied to the end of a precise chain of reasoning, such as the final answer to a complex mathematical equation or a set of formally defined propositions. For instance, if I propose that

  ○ All boys have red hair, and
  ○ Joe is a boy,

then deductive logic tells us that

○ Joe has red hair.

This deduction is an example of a *cognitive* process, meaning *thinking* in the sense of formal reasoning. The conclusion is said to "make sense" because is appeals to logic. Knowledge gained through rules of formal reasoning is said to be derived *logically*.

Of course, someone will eventually remind us that all boys do not really have red hair. The term *really* appeals to our understanding of the world as we perceive it through our five physical senses. Knowledge gained through our senses is said to be derived *empirically*.

At the risk of oversimplifying such rich disciplines as learning theory, psychology, logic, and any number of branches of metaphysics, I shall suggest that ideas derived either logically (through formal reasoning) or empirically (through one or more of our five senses) be classified within the general category of *cognitive* PIC techniques.

Some ideas seem to simply occur to us through some avenue we cannot describe, for example, intuition, inspiration, emotion, whimsy, faith, divine communication, extrasensory perception (senses other than our five empirical senses), and any number of other sources defying explicit description. I shall suggest that ideas derived from such sources be classified under the general category of *affective* PIC techniques.

Cognitive techniques appeal to the scientist in us. Affective techniques bring out our artistic qualities. Human beings are complex organisms, and bureaucracies are equally complex mixtures of human beings. It should hardly be surprising, therefore, to discover that creative thinking involves the use of both cognitive and affective faculties. Few creative enterprises are exclusively one or the other. Insight is an element of the scientific method, just as logic and perception are components of art. Nonetheless, the *primary* thrust of each included PIC technique is either cognitive or affective.

TECHNIQUES DESCRIPTIONS

Table 6-2 is a matrix showing which of the techniques described in this chapter are used to conduct each of the PIC phases, stages, and steps. Treat the table as a guide. Elements of techniques can be used in process steps in ways limited only by the imaginations of team members. But this table shows the primary PIC step focus for each technique.

Refer to Appendix III for a description of required **Teaming** facilities, equipment, and supplies.

Specific technique procedures are introduced in this chapter. Practical in-

TABLE 6-2 PIC: Techniques and Applications

	Process												
	1 Diagnosis						2 Prescriptions						
	1A Symptom Selection			1B Causes ID/Prioritization			2A Resolution(s) Selections			2B Implementation Planning			
Techniques	1A1 Symptom Speculation	1A2 Symptom Verification	1A3 Symptom Specification	1B1 C&R Speculation	1B2 C&R Verification	1B3 C&R Prioritization	2A1 Resolutions Speculation	2A2 Consequences Speculation	2A3 Resolutions Refinement	2B1 Scheduling Resources Speculation	2B2 Feasibility Verification	2B3 Action Item Speculation	2B4 Presentation
1.1 Divergence	×	×	×	×	×		×	×	×	×	×	×	
1.2 Convergence	×		×	×			×	×	×				
2 Stream Analysis	×		×										
3 C/E Diagramming				×									
4 Why–Because Pursuit				×									
5 Process Internalization				×		×							
6 Data/info Accumulation		×			×	×				×	×		×
7 How–By Pursuit							×						
8 Forcefield Diagramming								×					
9 Psychic Irrelevancy	×			×			×			×			

sights about their application within an actual team setting are offered in Chapter 7.

Refer to Table 5-3 as you read the following technique descriptions to refresh your understanding of the PIC. Refer to Table 6-1 to recall detailed outlines of PIC techniques. For purposes of simplicity, each technique is described below as if it is being conducted by a facilitator for individuals who are learning the process and techniques for the first time.

1. DIVERGENCE/CONVERGENCE (D/C)

Divergence/convergence is the most pervasive technique used during the PIC. It appears, in whole or in part, during every PIC step. It is also used in conjunction with some of the other techniques.

Divergence exercises cognitive and affective faculties almost equally, the balance depending on the character of the issue under consideration. Convergence is primarily cognitive.

Divergence is the act of generating as many ideas as possible with respect to some stated area of interest. For instance, assume that a department head has been receiving complaints from personnel about the use of office computers. Complaints vary across a wide spectrum. The manager convenes ten people in the conference room, composed of those who have complained and those who know most about computer capabilities. Their charge is to find and solve whatever problems exist with respect to office automation. They are, in effect, entering the PIC at Step 1A1, **Symptom Speculation** (see Table 5-3). Another team might be given a specific symptom statement and asked to determine its causes. For instance, the given statement might be, "Computer terminals are not available when needed." They would be entering the PIC at Step 1B1, **C&R Speculation.** Both teams will Diverge/Converge (D/C). The second team will also use additional techniques specified in Table 6-2 for Step 1B1.

Convergence is the act of prioritizing or ranking ideas generated during divergence. The purpose is to identify the one or few explicit statement(s) (from out of the total generated) that most appropriately specify, by general consensus, the desired issue(s). For instance, the second team wants to identify the few most significant causes for computer unavailability, while the first team desires to isolate the one most crucial office computer problem, from out of the pack, to attack first.

1.1 Divergence

1.1.1 Nominal Group Technique (NGT)

Features

Nominal Group Technique (NGT) is a private divergence technique. Brainstorming is public. I personally find NGT most satisfying as a thinking stimulator. It lets people go off into their own relaxing mental corner for a few moments of quiet contemplation. It also provides anonymity for people who would prefer that the source of their ideas remain confidential, at least temporarily, for any number of private reasons.

Procedures (Figure 6-1)*

○ Hang flip chart sheet on the wall (prior to beginning of the session).
   ○○ Provide enough to accommodate five or six ideas per sheet.
○ Distribute two or three 3 by 5 inch cards to members.
   ○○ Two cards if nine or more people.
   ○○ Three cards if eight or fewer people.
○ Instruct members to write one, and only one, idea on each card.
○ No talking.
   ○○ Cautions:
      ○○○ *Print* neatly.
      ○○○ Use either pen or dark pencil.
      ○○○ Be brief . . . no essays . . . suggest 10 words or less as general guideline.
      ○○○ Set a time limit (5 to 10 minutes), but do not push someone for the difference of a few moments (good time for a working break).
      ○○○ Ask everyone to retain cards until everyone has completed the task.
○ Collect and shuffle cards (for anonymity).
○ Ask for volunteers to write entries on flip chart sheets hung on wall, one person per sheet.
   ○○ Give volunteers the same dark color marker, for example, black, brown, blue, violet (save bright colors for later convergence markings).
   ○○ Rules:
      ○○○ No talking
      ○○○ No more than six ideas per sheet, evenly spaced with about 6 to 8 inches between entries.
      ○○○ Do not number ideas.
      ○○○ Establish a 6-inch left margin and draw a bullet on that margin at the beginning of each entry.
      ○○○ *Absolutely no editing.* Write each entry *exactly* as written on card, including spelling and/or syntax errors
      ○○○ *Be neat.* Remember, people must be able to read the entries from their seats.

*Note: This divergent NGT procedure is described as if it is being conducted excluding combinations with any other technique, such as Cause and Effect diagramming or Why–Because pursuit.

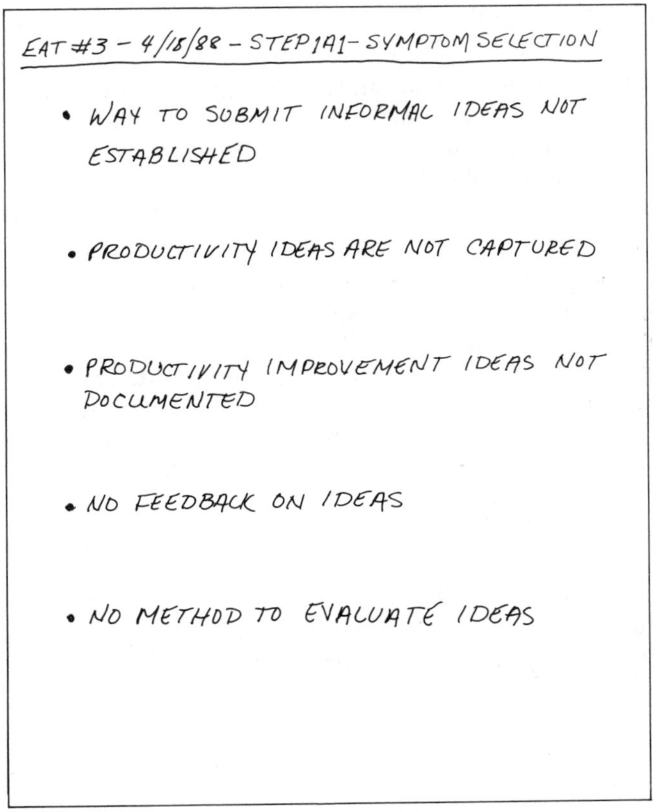

EAT #3 — 4/18/88 — STEP 1A1 — SYMPTOM SELECTION

- WAY TO SUBMIT INFORMAL IDEAS NOT ESTABLISHED

- PRODUCTIVITY IDEAS ARE NOT CAPTURED

- PRODUCTIVITY IMPROVEMENT IDEAS NOT DOCUMENTED

- NO FEEDBACK ON IDEAS

- NO METHOD TO EVALUATE IDEAS

Figure 6-1 Typical Flip Chart Sheet: Divergent NGT

ooo Volunteers return cards and markers to facilitator or specified central area when sheet completed and return to seat.

ooo Individuals at table should read entries as they are being written on sheets.

oooo Search for surprising ideas.

oooo Try to think of additional ideas that are inspired by what you are reading.

oooo Write any newly inspired ideas on a sheet of paper for later entry.

o Await directions to begin new technique

The most striking aspect of NGT divergence, to the newcomer, is the speed with which 20 to 30 ideas are generated and recorded for all to see, within the space of 10 or 15 minutes. I always ask initiates what their reaction would have been if I had given each of them 10 or 15 minutes to come up with 20 to 30 original ideas on the subject of concern. They recognize, immediately, the low probability of successful performance on that request.

1.1.2 Brainstorming (Figure 6-2)

Brainstorming's great virtue is that it allows (in fact, demands) individuals to generate a continuous chain of new ideas on insights gained by building on what peers have to say. It is a symbiotic activity. Properly conducted, brainstorming establishes a rhythm of linked statement generation that captures participants' imaginations in a flowing tide of new ideas. It is not a solitary endeavor. Each individual must listen carefully to what is being said and "grab" insights inspired by the chain of ideas circling the room. In this sense, brainstorming is very much an affective technique.

Random brainstorming is conducted by allowing everyone to state an idea as soon as it occurs to them. Each person simply shouts it out. The scribe writes the idea on flip chart sheets as fast as possible, being careful to record it accurately. The process is disorderly, but not chaotic. It works best when flashes of insight are being sought, that is when affective faculties are called on, such as in technique 9, *Psychic Irrelevancy.*

Structured brainstorming is conducted in an orderly sequence. Each person offers one idea per turn. Turns move from individual to individual in a continuous, unbroken flow around the room. The process is as much cognitive as it is affective. Each individual carefully considers the flow of ideas and develops new entries for contribution during subsequent turns. I tend to favor this form

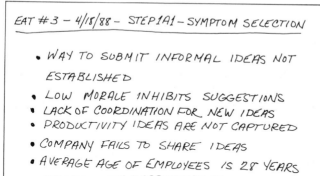

Figure 6-2 Typical Flip Chart Sheet: Brainstorming Added

during most of the PIC steps, but this is a personal inclination. Team members can set their own rules regarding when to use either form of brainstorming.

Regardless of the form used, do not fool yourself into thinking that groups of people are brainstorming simply by offering *isolated* individual ideas within a collective setting. If they are ignoring each others' contributions, then (by my standards) they are not brainstorming. They are simply recording isolated individual thoughts. It is the holistic character of the process that make it so very powerful . . . individuals joining their intellects into a network of ideas accelerated to new heights by the energy of collective reinforcements. *E pluribus unum! Many as one!*

Procedures

1.1.2.1 Random Brainstorming

- ○ Individuals call out ideas as they occur to them.
- ○ Facilitator or scribe writes ideas on flip chart sheets.
  - ○○ Add entries on wall-hung sheets, if continuing from NGT divergence, or if the brainstorming is being conducted as part of another technique employing specialized diagramming, for example fishbone diagramming or HOW–BY Pursuit.
  - ○○ Enter ideas at top of a new sheet if beginning divergence with brainstorming and no other technique's specialized diagramming is being used.
  - ○○ Rules:
    - ○○○ Observe simple rules of courtesy to prevent chaos . . . ideas traffic can become congested.
    - ○○○ Individuals listen carefully to flow of ideas and let new thoughts develop from them.
    - ○○○ Individuals read ideas as they are written on the sheets (visual cues strike us differently than audio cues and we can increase our insights by using both perceptual faculties).
    - ○○○ No additional talking or comments about entries.
    - ○○○ All ideas are acceptable . . . no idea is absurd.
- ○ Process ends when no one has an idea to offer.
  - ○○ Do not stop even if only one person is continuing.
  - ○○ Do not make that person self-conscious about holding up events.
  - ○○ The last ideas could be the best ideas.
  - ○○ Those last few ideas could rekindle a whole new set of ideas in other peoples' minds.
  - ○○ Early completion is not the object of the exercise; full expression of ideas is the object.

1.1.2.2 Structured Brainstorming

○ Random brainstorming rules hold, except as noted below:
  ○○ No talking except during turn.
  ○○ No killer phrases or body language to intimidate individuals.
  ○○ Rotate turn either clockwise or counterclockwise.
  ○○ One idea per turn.
  ○○ Do *not* stop flow of process.
  ○○ Must say "pass," if:
    ○○○ Nothing to contribute during turn.
      ○○○○ Ensures individual is participating.
      ○○○○ Stimulates listening and thinking.
      ○○○○ Important for peers to know person is listening.
      ○○○○ Courtesy to next person in line.
    ○○○ Not sure how to state idea.
      ○○○○ Compose idea on sheet of paper for next turn.
      ○○○○ Do *not* ask peers to help with phrasing.
        ○○○○○ Interrupts flow.
        ○○○○○ Disturbs individual thoughts.
        ○○○○○ Ideas are lost.
○ Try to hold any questions about the brainstorming process, itself, until it is completed.
  ○○ Interrupts thinking.
  ○○ Ideas are lost.
○ Process ends when everyone passes.
  ○○ Circle room twice for passes.
  ○○ Encourage person with last few ideas.
    ○○○ Whole new round could be stimulated by one final statement.
    ○○○ Squeeze out every last idea.

The session formally ends when one member so moves and there are no objections. Remember that there is no seconding, or "the ayes have it," in PIC **Teaming**. Majorities count for nothing . . . there must be full consensus on any motion. Therefore, the proper response to the motion is for the facilitator or team leader to say: "We have a motion to close brainstorming. Are there any objections?" If there are no objections, then the activity ends. But, if just one person objects, then the activity continues.

This rule is not arbitrary. Remember that consensus is lost if one person is intimidated or forced to go along with the group. That person has been denied choice, the one thing that cannot be tolerated. If consensus is lost during any step of the PIC, the price will be failure at the end. The seeds of failure can lay dormant through several steps and even stages . . . the longer the worse. Its consequences multiply because later decisions are based on earlier false consensuses. The results can be demoralizing. If the truth is suppressed until the presentation of results to managers or sponsors, they will surely ask questions that will eventually uncover the latent divisions among team members. The results can be personally and organizationally devastating. Take my word for it . . . you do not want to learn this lesson the hard way.

1.2 Convergence

Features

Convergence is ranking. The idea is to select (by consensus) the few (or one) best ideas from out of the population of total ideas generated during divergence. The technique is best introduced by looking at its component steps backward (refer to Table 6-1, items 1.2.1 to 1.2.5). The last step in convergence is to vote (item 1.2.5). But this is not the familiar kind of "one-vote-majority-wins" kind of balloting most of us have experienced. We are looking for consensus. Consensus voting requires many elimination ballots. It is something like the Miss America Pageant. The winner is not selected when all the contestants appear on the stage for the first time. Numerous rounds of voting take place to eliminate individuals, leaving an ever smaller population of candidates eligible for the next round of voting. Early ballots focus on eliminations. Later ballots focus on ranking finalists. The three listed voting techniques are designed for just this kind of multiple balloting.

But before members vote, it is only fair to give each of them the opportunity to influence their peers' votes, that is, to convince others to vote for certain ideas listed on the sheets. Therefore, before voting, everyone gets this opportunity during the lobbying part of convergence.

But why lobby and vote for ideas until their language has been simplified and clarified? Remember that the entries on the sheet were the product of individual thoughts generated as they occurred. They might not be worded as clearly as possible and might not accurately convey the authors' true meaning. Therefore, they must be clarified sufficiently for members to know what they are voting for. Several of the diverged entries might say the same thing in different words. Why should members have to vote for the same idea more than one time? To prevent such redundant behavior, members are given the opportunity to combine like ideas before voting. They also get a chance to add, delete and/or modify listed entries. This phase of the convergence technique is titled *CDAM* (combine, delete, add, modify). Prior to these actions, the entries are sequentially numbered.

Procedures

1.2.1 Numbering (Figure 6-3)

○ Number entries (1 to N) sequentially.
○ Refer to entries by number throughout convergence.

1.2.2 Clarifying (Figure 6-4)

○ Ask the author of each entry to give a short explanation of the essential meaning of the statement.
○ Ask members if further clarification is required.
○ Rules:
    ○○ Statement belongs to the author until clarifying is completed.
    ○○ No discussions; intent is to ensure that everyone *understands* author's meaning and intent.
    ○○ Not necessary for members to agree with the statement.
    ○○ Author can change wording as desired to further clarify own statement.
    ○○ Review every statement or have individuals ask for specific clarifications if number of entries is very large.

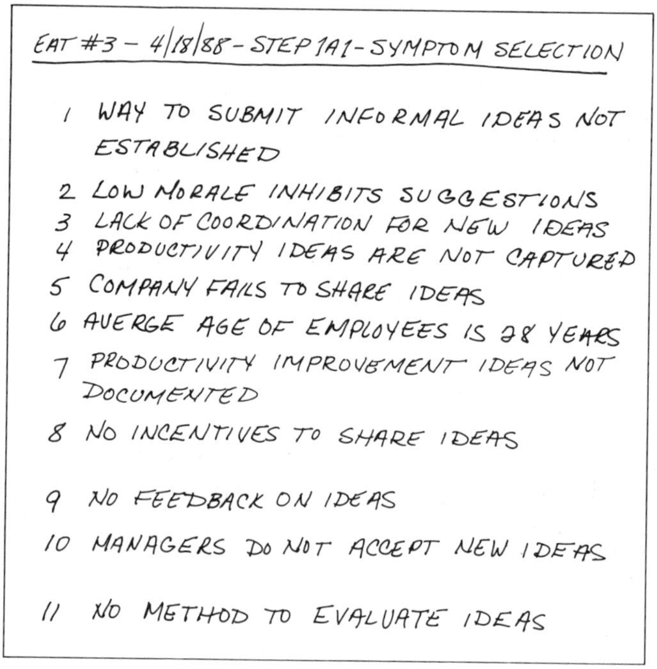

EAT #3 – 4/18/88 – STEP 1A1 – SYMPTOM SELECTION

1 WAY TO SUBMIT INFORMAL IDEAS NOT ESTABLISHED
2 LOW MORALE INHIBITS SUGGESTIONS
3 LACK OF COORDINATION FOR NEW IDEAS
4 PRODUCTIVITY IDEAS ARE NOT CAPTURED
5 COMPANY FAILS TO SHARE IDEAS
6 AVERGE AGE OF EMPLOYEES IS 28 YEARS
7 PRODUCTIVITY IMPROVEMENT IDEAS NOT DOCUMENTED
8 NO INCENTIVES TO SHARE IDEAS
9 NO FEEDBACK ON IDEAS
10 MANAGERS DO NOT ACCEPT NEW IDEAS
11 NO METHOD TO EVALUATE IDEAS

Figure 6-3 Typical Flip Chart Sheet: Convergence Numbering

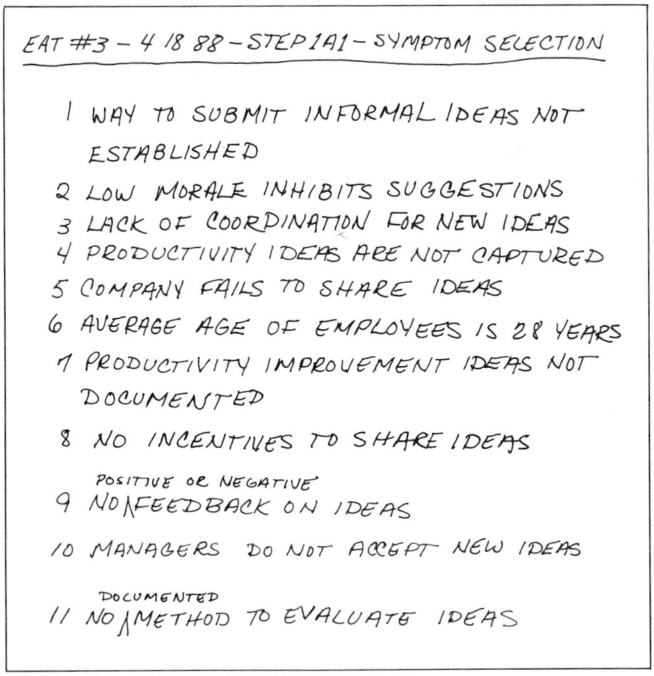

EAT #3 – 4 /8 88 – STEP 1A1 – SYMPTOM SELECTION

1 WAY TO SUBMIT INFORMAL IDEAS NOT
  ESTABLISHED
2 LOW MORALE INHIBITS SUGGESTIONS
3 LACK OF COORDINATION FOR NEW IDEAS
4 PRODUCTIVITY IDEAS ARE NOT CAPTURED
5 COMPANY FAILS TO SHARE IDEAS
6 AVERAGE AGE OF EMPLOYEES IS 28 YEARS
7 PRODUCTIVITY IMPROVEMENT IDEAS NOT
  DOCUMENTED
8 NO INCENTIVES TO SHARE IDEAS
  POSITIVE OR NEGATIVE
9 NO FEEDBACK ON IDEAS
10 MANAGERS DO NOT ACCEPT NEW IDEAS
   DOCUMENTED
11 NO METHOD TO EVALUATE IDEAS

Figure 6-4 Typical Flip Chart Sheet: Convergence Clarification

oo Clarification can be reopened at any time during subsequent convergence phases, but should be completed as much as possible at this time.

1.2.3 CDAM (Figure 6-5)

1.2.3.1 Combining

o Purpose is to simplify voting.
o Select any *two* statements that seem to say the same thing.
  oo Decide which of them would make the better lead statement.
  oo Refer to the statements by their respective numbers.
  oo Recommend that the two seemingly similar statements be combined in the following words: "I recommend that number '11' be combined under number '7.'" The second number "7" is the "lead" statement.
o If no objections, then the scribe writes the combination on the flip chart sheets, as shown in Figure 6-3 (combining number 11 under number 7).
  oo Cross out the identifying number of the statement being moved (number 11).
  oo Write that number under the text of the lead statement (number 7), at the left edge of the text, in parentheses.

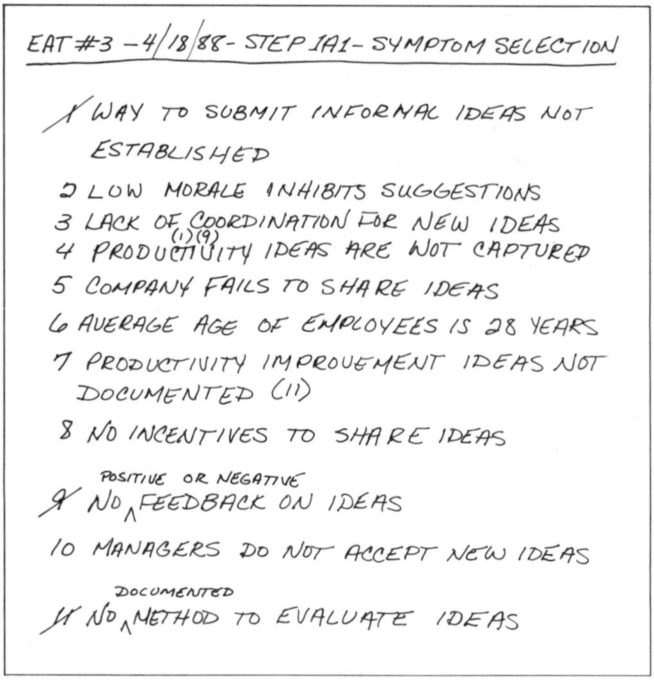

Figure 6-5 Typical Flip Chart Sheet: Convergence Combining

○ Rules:
  ○○ Any number of statements can be combined under one statement, but only one combination can be recommended at a time.
  ○○ Allow recommendations to be made randomly.
  ○○ If one person objects to any recommendation, then the combination is canceled.
  ○○ Objecting person should simply say, "Objection".
  ○○ No discussion allowed concerning objection.
    ○○○ Objection simply means that the objector believes that the two statements are distinct and different enough to warrant separate votes.
    ○○○ Objecting is *not* a negative act and the facilitator must remind participants of this fact.
    ○○○ Objections to combinations are accepted without discussion because *individual choice* is the most important factor to preserve, and no person should be forced to implicitly vote for any statement simply because it is combined with some other statement that he or she wishes to choose.
    ○○○ When in doubt about a recommended combination, I suggest an objection because the convenience of simplified voting is not as important as preserving individual choice during voting.

1.2.3.2 Deleting (Figure 6-6)

○ Delete statements that appear to be irrelevant to the topic.
○ Do *not* delete statements in lieu of combining them under similar statements.
  ○○ It is important during voting to see how many times the same idea has been suggested.
  ○○ Different versions of the same idea add nuances that are important if a statement (and its combined partners) are chosen for further consideration.
○ Rules:
  ○○ Anyone can suggest a deletion.
  ○○ One objection stops the deletion; no explanation required.
  ○○ Best guideline for deletion is consensus that the statement is totally irrelevant to the topic (number "6").

1.2.3.3 Adding (Figure 6-7)

○ Adding is conducted similarly to random brainstorming (see number "12").
○ Rules:

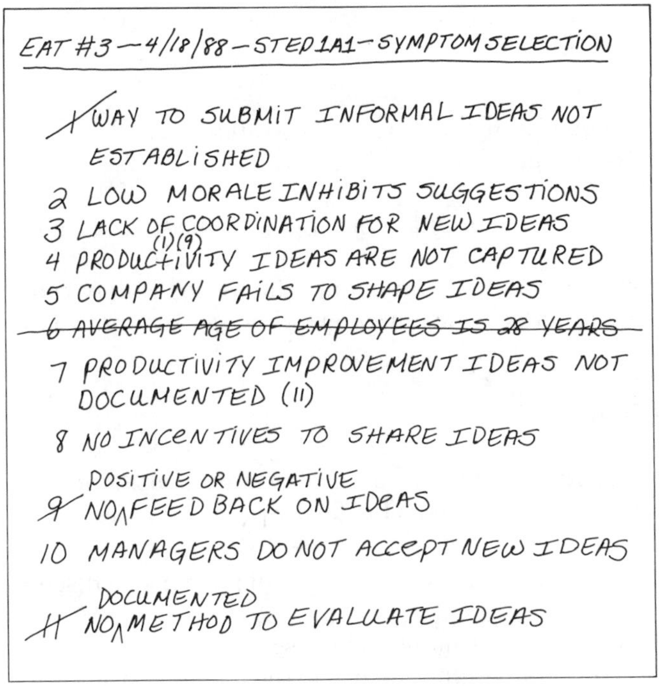

Figure 6-6 Typical Flip Chart Sheet: Convergence Deleting

Figure 6-7 Typical Flip Chart Sheet: Convergence Adding

○○ Anyone can add a statement.
○○ Number additions sequentially with existing statements.
○○ No one can object to an addition.
○○ Clarify all additions.
○○ Additions are eligible for combining, deleting, and modifying along with all other entries.
○○ Adding is a good way to combine statements that seem to defy combining, but require only a generic statement that can accommodate all of them.

1.2.3.4 Modifying (Figure 6-8)

○ Anyone can suggest a change in the wording of a statement, since all statements are collectively owned after clarification (see number "7")
○ Rules:
  ○○ State the desired change succinctly, without explanations or discussion.
  ○○ Make the change in wording if no one objects.
  ○○ If someone objects, the change must be discussed; the objection does not automatically carry in this case.

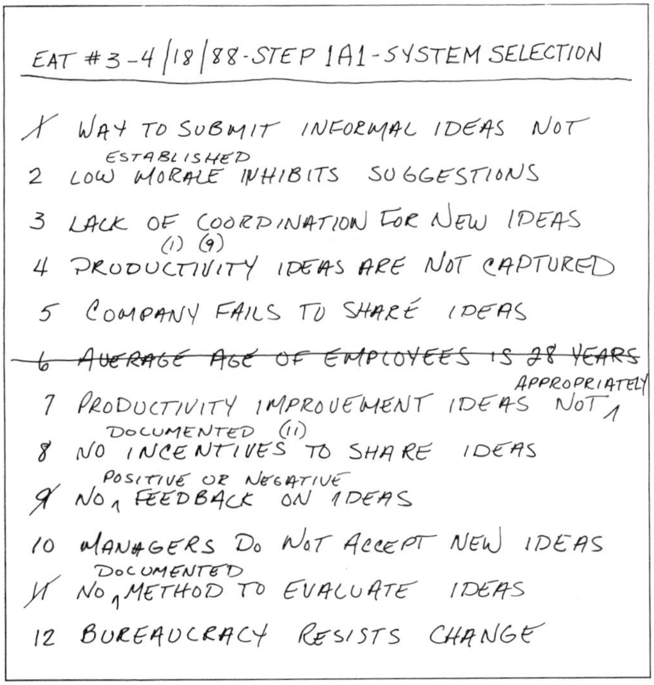

Figure 6-8 Typical Flip Chart Sheet: Convergence Modifying

oo Rules for discussion:

  ooo Do *not* debate your disagreement over the wording; this is what causes meetings to break down.

  ooo Concentrate on what you *agree on*, for instance, the original statement was originally accepted by everyone.

  ooo Start discussion by asking the suggestor to briefly explain the reason for the suggested modification.

  ooo Objectors must listen carefully to and seriously consider the reasons for the modification.

  ooo If more than one objector, get consensus between suggestor and first objector before going on to the other objections.

  ooo Objector, after seriously considering the suggestor's reasons for the change, gives a short explanation for the objection.

  ooo *Remember*, the object is to find a common ground, not to stick stubbornly to "my" interpretation.

  If no consensus after explanations, each person should again concentrate on the areas of agreement and determine the, usually very minor, spot of disagreement.

  ooo Each person should ask himself or herself the following questions: "What could the other person say that would turn me to accept his or her interpretation?" Or "How could the wording be changed to accommodate both of our meanings?" *Listen! Empathize! Seek accommodation without sacrificing your intent!*

ooo If no accommodation is found, one person should simply add a new statement and both statements can stand.

ooo Seek advice from other team members; they usually can find the appropriate words to satisfy both persons because they are apart from the debate.

ooo *Repeat* . . . seek a working consensus that *satisfies*, that each individual can accept and that enjoys general acceptance.

o At the end of CDAM, circle the *numbers only* of those statements remaining as candidates for voting.

1.2.4 Lobbying

o Before voting each individual has a chance to explain his or her preferences.

o Object is to suggest reasons for peers to vote for your preferences.

o Rules:

oo Must lobby for a statement . . . with positive tone.

oo Must *never* lobby against a statement . . . with negative tone . . . immediately puts someone else on the defensive.

oo Suggest a random lobby, that is, a person simply calls out, "I want to lobby for number X because . . ." (keep it brief).

oo Lobby for as many items as you wish, but only one per turn.

oo Lobbies supporting previous lobbies are perfectly reasonable and permitted.

oo If lobbies are confusing, ask for reclarification of the entry in question by the original author.

oo *Do not argue, debate or discuss . . . just listen and make your own choices.*

1.2.5 Voting

Remember that we seek consensus, not majority winners and minority losers. We desire a 100 percent *satisficing* consensus on which of the alternative statements are the best statements with respect to the issue under consideration. Therefore, each person must have a *chance* to vote, at least once, for every statement, that is, there must be "multi" (many) voting ballots. Succeeding ballots are arranged for elimination voting, very much like the Miss America Contest, where in the first round 50 plus women appear on the stage. The winner is not selected by one ballot of one vote per judge. Instead, a series of elimination ballots are taken to winnow the population down to semifinalists and finalists, who are then ranked to determine the runners up and final winner.

Considering that, in any given PIC step, the initial population of statements can grow to over 200 alternatives, the value of all the preceding convergence techniques becomes obvious. The intense and repeated deliberations conducted between numbering and voting allow people to develop ever more sophisticated understandings and opinions about the relative worth of statements. After a few excursions through the entire divergence/convergence exercise, individuals and teams become expert at the process and conduct it with mutual trust, empathy, and ease. It is very user friendly.

Of the three voting techniques to be discussed, only multivoting is usable for balloting on 20 or more alternatives. Convergent NGT works best with 20 or fewer alternatives, and discrete summation loses favor with more than 10 remaining choices. Multivoting works regardless of the number of alternatives, from two to hundreds. The ranking of finalists typically occurs when 20 or fewer alternatives remain and different individuals usually favor one of the three techniques at this time. But it is seldom difficult to gain consensus on one. In fact, individuals usually enjoy trying all three techniques during votes conducted in subsequent PIC steps.

Sometimes the mechanics of one technique do not produce a real sense of satisfying consensus among members. The numbers on the sheets indicate ranking, but the spirit of agreement is clearly missing. A change of technique often changes that unhappy result. If this does not work, then the team must go back to some previous convergence step, for example, clarifying, CDAM, or lobbying, and work its way back to voting for finalists. As always, the answer to a roadblock in the activity is to let the process set you free (see Shuster's Law #7).

The probabilites are that voting will begin with 40 or more statements remaining as available choices after CDAM and lobbying. Therfore, multivoting will be used to eliminate the alternative having little or no chance to become finalists. The process is the same regardless of whether the particular PIC step being conducted requires choosing just one item, such as Symptom Specification (PIC Step 1A3), or more than one item, such as Causes and Roots Speculation (PIC Step 1B1). In the latter case, the number of causes that will finally be chosen need not be predetermined. The mechanics of the voting techniques will draw that final number out as a reflection of the consensus in the room. Voting, then, is a discovery exercise. The underlying consensus in the room is discovered through the mechanics of the voting techiniques.

1.2.5.1 Multivoting

Features

Multivoting is a public form of convergence voting. Members vote for available remaining statements by raising their hands as the statement numbers are called. After all the votes are called, counted, and recorded, a decision is made, through consensus, regarding which statements should be eliminated for the next round of voting. This seems straightforward enough. But the real power of multivoting is found in a few vital rules that make it a true reflection of consensus, rather than simply a summation of individual choices.

The first vital rule regulates the number of alternatives individuals can vote for during each round of voting. Basically, this restriction can be summarized as:

Round 1: Rule of all

Round 2: Rule of halves

During the first round of voting, each individual can vote, *once*, for every candidate statement. Therefore, if the initial number of candidates is 52, then each member can vote for as few as zero, all 52, or some number in between. This guarantees that no member will ever be in the position of lacking an opportunity to express a choice. Remember that in consensus building expression of individual choice is the glue that cements unity. Therefore, at the conclusion of the first round, those statements that received zero or only a few votes can truly be viewed as lacking general favor. During the first round of voting, then, choices are free. No one is required to give up a vote for one statement as a price to pay for choosing an alternative.

During the second and subsequent rounds of voting (however many are required), voting is preceded by a consensus decision about which alternatives should be eliminated as candidates. Understand that the term "elimination" does not mean "destroy." Remember the dictum that in the PIC nothing is ever lost. Even items deleted during CDAM were not obiterated. They were simply removed from contention "at that time." One learns very quickly in the PIC that ideas have a way of rising, phoenixlike, from irrelevance in one step to pertinence in some subsequent step. However, once the elimination process for the second voting round is completed, the number of remaining candidates is counted and the *rule of halves* is involved. Simply put, each member can vote for a *maximum* of one-half of the remaining candidates. If the number of remaining alternatives is 34, then each person can vote for as few as zero, as many as 17 (one half of 34), or some number in between. If there is an odd number of remaining alternatives, then the number of votes is to be one-half of either the next higher or next lower even number. I prefer the next lower even number because one must prioritize that much more carefully and think that much more critically with one less available choice. But that is my personal preference. Group consensus determines this issue.

In fact, the rule of halves is, itself, a matter of consensus. It could just as easily be a rule of three-quarters or a rule of two-fifths. I recommend the rule of halves because of hard experience. Mechanically, it seems to fit well with inherent senses of fairness and with individual efforts to evaluate priorities. But its real value is in what it prevents. And that is the waste of time and good energy that team members begin to sense over an issue of relatively trivial moment. It becomes very obvious very quickly that the rule should provide enough candidate statements to allow fruitful choice and should, simultaneously, restrict candidates to a population small enough to stimulate careful individual evaluation, prioritization and ranking. If ever a golden mean for cooperative behavior existed, the rule of halves in this situation must surely be it.

The mechanics of voting in the second and subsequent rounds is the same as for round 1. Hands are raised for each candidate and votes are counted and recorded. How many rounds of voting are required? There is no set number. Each episode of multivoting is unique in this regard. But the principle underlying the determination of number of voting rounds is expressed in the second vital rule that makes multivoting a true reflection of consensus.

The second vital rule establishes the subtle shift in individual mind-sets that occurs as each episode of multivoting progresses from start to finish. The two mind-sets should be:

Initial Rounds: Eliminate Non-Finalists
Late Rounds: Rank/Prioritize Finalists

Regardless of whether a particular episode of multivoting is aiming toward one or a few end choices, the initial rounds express a quality of getting rid of alternatives. But, as these elimination rounds progress, certain statements begin to visibly exhibit a character of *staying power* that implies their near certainty as finalists. When this occurs depends on the number of initial candidates: what PIC phase/stage/step is being conducted, the character of the issue under consideration, results of previous verification steps and many other variables. My experience indicates that semifinalists begin to appear when about 15 to 25 candidates remain, and the finalists emerge with about 5 to 10 surviving alternatives. The facilitator or leader should be cognizant of this shift and point out its virtues as questions arise about voting procedures.

Throughout the multivoting episode questions such as "can I ask for further clarification on number 'X'" "can I recommend more combinations," or "can I modify number 'X,'" can very probably arise. The answer should, with few exceptions, be "yes." But, as always, it is up to team consensus. Be prepared, however, to bear later costs for early impatience. Consider the third vital rule making multivoting a true reflection of consensus. I call it the *Rule of Recapitulation*:

ALLOW REOPENINGS OF PREVIOUS CONVERGENCE TECHNIQUES *BETWEEN* INDIVIDUAL ROUNDS OF MULTIVOTING.

It should be obvious at this point that the entire convergence process, from numbering of statements through voting, is a critical thinking and learning exercise. As people probe into the subject and ideas fly around the table, a synthesis of understanding occurs in every mind and sophistication of insight opens doors to perspectives that earlier were unobtainable. Therefore, the mood in the room should be conducive ... even eager ... to welcome a new arrangement of candidates that might remove a roadblock to prioritizing finalists and resolving individual uncertainties.

The one limit I suggest is that recapitulation be allowed only between rounds of voting and not during a round. Constant interruptions of voting cloud thinking and tend to create growing impatience and irritation ... for obvious reasons. But, as always, such a limit is a matter of group consensus. Better to learn the hard way and agree than to suffer imposed constraints.

Multivoting ends at one of two junctures. First, it ends when the final single choice or multiple choices have been selected. Second, it ends at or near the finalist stage and there is a consensus to end voting by using convergent NGT or discrete summation. Convergent NGT works best with 12 to 20 remaining candidates. Discrete summation is most suited to 3 to 10 alternatives. I know of no general rule for deciding which technique to choose during the end game. Let consensus decide. However, I can suggest that the best way out of the impasse that sometimes occurs when the mechanical voting technique employed fails to satisfy the underlying sense of consensus is to shift techniques. If that fails, then somewhere in the convergent process, before voting, consensus was missed. The team must go back and retrieve it. In fact, consensus might really have been lost during some early step, stage, or phase of the PIC, itself. Whatever the case, backtracking and consensus retrieval are the only answers. As stated in **Shuster's Law #7**, only the process can set you free.

Procedures (Figures 6-9, 6-10)

○ Facilitator/leader/scribe draws a blank voting grid with a felt pen on flip chart sheet(s) prior to voting period (as shown in Figure 6-9).
  ○○ Grid space density should be about 18 columns by 25 rows.
  ○○ Label the top of sheet for later identification with the following data:
    ○○○ Team name or number.
    ○○○ PIC step, for example, 1B1.
    ○○○ Title, for example, *Multivote*.
    ○○○ Name of any other special technique during which the convergence is being conducted, for example, "Cause and Effect Diagram," or "WHY– BECAUSE Pursuit 1."
    ○○○ Total number of people voting.
○ Facilitator/leader/scribe enters into the grid the numbers of the candidate statements remaining after CDAM and lobbying.
  ○○ They are the statements whose identifying numbers were circled at the end of CDAM.
  ○○ Enter the numbers in numerical sequence beginning in column 1, row 1 (1,1).

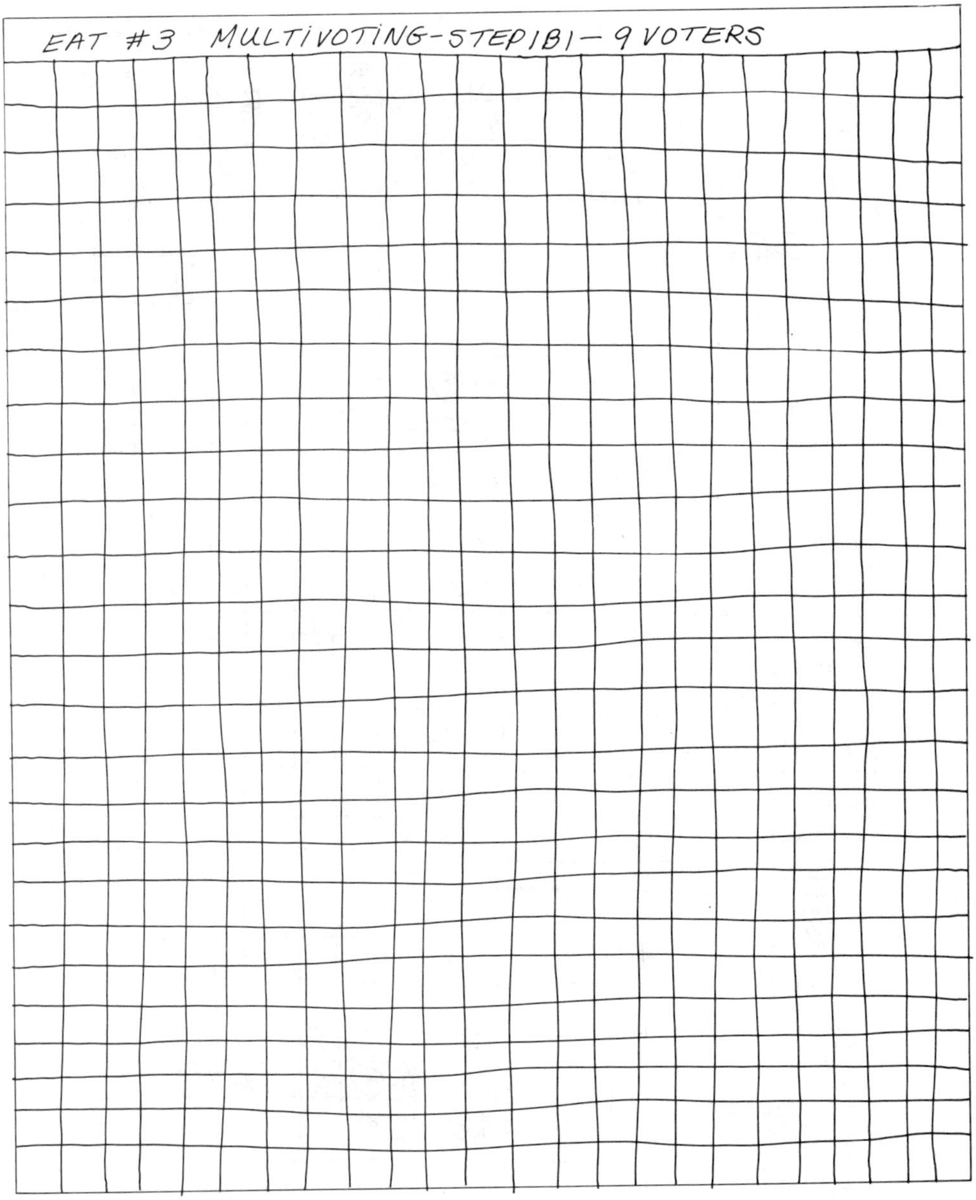

EAT #3 MULTIVOTING-STEP|B|— 9 VOTERS

Figure 6-9   Typical Blank Flip Chart Sheet: Convergence Multivoting

oo Continue entering candidate numbers down the first column, to the last row, that is space 1, 25.

oo Enter the next numbers in column 10, beginning with space 10, 1 and proceeding to 10, 25.

   ooo This leaves enough columns for eight rounds of voting, that is, one column per round per candidate.

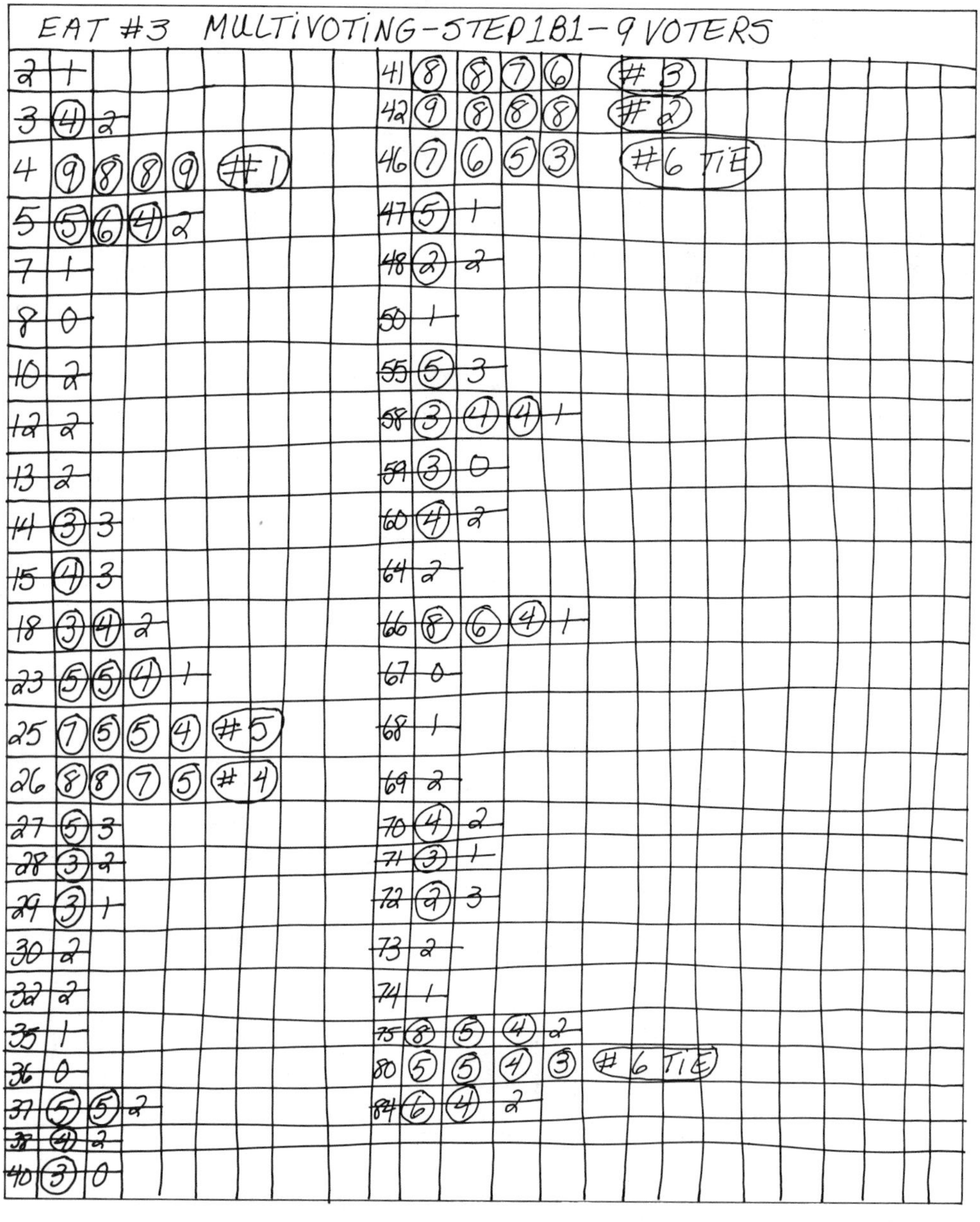

EAT #3   MULTIVOTING—STEP 1B1— 9 VOTERS

#					
2	1				
3	(4)	2			
4	(9)	(8)	(8)	(9)	#1
5	(5)	(6)	(4)	2	
7	1				
8	0				
10	2				
12	2				
13	2				
14	(3)	3			
15	(4)	3			
18	(3)	(4)	2		
23	(5)	(5)	(4)	1	
25	(7)	(5)	(5)	(4)	#5
26	(8)	(8)	(7)	(5)	#4
27	(5)	3			
28	(3)	2			
29	(3)	1			
30	2				
32	2				
35	1				
36	0				
37	(5)	(5)	2		
38	(4)	2			
40	(3)	0			
41	(8)	(8)	(7)	(6)	#3
42	(9)	(8)	(8)	(8)	#2
46	(7)	(6)	(5)	(3)	#6 TIE
47	(5)	1			
48	(2)	2			
50	1				
55	(5)	3			
58	(3)	(4)	(4)	1	
59	(3)	0			
60	(4)	2			
64	2				
66	(8)	(6)	(4)	1	
67	0				
68	1				
69	2				
70	(4)	2			
71	(3)	1			
72	(9)	3			
73	2				
74	1				
75	(8)	(5)	(4)	2	
80	(5)	(5)	(4)	(3)	#6 TIE
84	(6)	(4)	2		

Figure 6-10   Typical Flip Chart Sheet: Convergence Multivoting

ooo Use a second flip chart grid sheet if more than 50 candidates exist.

o Each individual team member takes a clean sheet of paper and sequentially lists the candidate statement numbers in columns.

○ Individuals take 5 to 10 minutes to determine which candidate state-
   ments they intend to vote for during the first round of voting.
   ○○ Facilitator/leader ensures that everyone understands the *Rule of All*
      for the first round of voting.
      ○○○ Since, under the rule, choices are free, then you (as a voter)
          should feel free to vote for any candidate even if you feel that it is
          low on your priority list as a finalist in subsequent voting
          rounds.
      ○○○ Do not vote for those candidates that you reject.
   ○○ Circle the identifying numbers of those, and only those, candidates
      that you intend to vote for in round 1.
   ○○ Allow additional time for personal consideration. *Do not rush people.*
      True consensus is the goal, not a savings of 5 to 10 minutes.
   ○○ No talking.
○ If the facilitator is scribing, then he or she can call out the candidate
   numbers, count the raised hands for each candidate, and enter the voting
   totals for each candidate.
   ○○ Since the facilitator does not participate, this function is relatively
      easy to perform.
   ○○ If no facilitator is present, then the team must appoint a caller/
      counter and a scribe.
      ○○○ Since they are participants, they must pay very careful attention
          to their split responsibilities or they will make mistakes.
      ○○○ Other team members should help them as much as possible.
○ When everyone is prepared to vote, the facilitator gives the following in-
   structions:
   ○○ When a number is called, those voting for it must raise one hand,
      high, and keep it there until the total count is called.
      ○○○ Do not raise hands halfway.
      ○○○ Do not drop hands early.
      ○○○ Those rejecting the statement must be careful about moving
          arms in such a way as to cause facilitator to count it as a vote, for
          example, scratching head, leaning back with arms behind head.
   ○○ No talking.
○ Facilitator begins round by calling out the first candidate number.
   ○○ Counts raised hands.
   ○○ Enters the sum total in column two, space 2,1.
   ○○ Continues the process until votes are entered for each candidate, at
      which point the voting round ends.
○ Facilitator asks the following question:
   ○○ "Are there any recommendations for dropping (eliminating) candi-
      dates for the next round of voting?"
      ○○○ Instructs members that they should consider, in their own
          minds, the minimum number of received votes that should qual-
          ify candidates for survival into the next round of voting.

○○○○ Pure numbers of votes received are not the sole criterion members can use. They should also consider the importance of statements that might be dropped if any given numerical threshold for rejection is defined.

○○○○ Such considerations will vary as the voting rounds progress.

○○ Explains that the appropriate language for recommending candidate elimination is:

○○○ "I recommend that, for the next round of voting, all candidates receiving a vote of 'X' (for example, '3' or less) be dropped."

○○ If no one objects, then the list of available voting candidate statements is reduced by eliminating those that receive a vote of "X" votes or less.

○○○○ Someone might object by stating, "I object and recommend dropping those receiving 'X – 1' votes or less (for example, '2' votes or less) instead of the originally recommended '3' votes or less."

○○○○ If that is the only objection raised, then members are obliged to accept the lower number (2 votes or less) because the objector would lose choices if the higher reject value were accepted.

○○○○ Perfectly reasonable for the team to accept dropping all candidates with "X" votes or less, while exempting one (or a few) that a member feels strongly about. For example, "I recommend dropping candidates with '2,' or less votes with the exceptions of numbers 48 and 72" (which both have '2' votes).

○○○○ Principle is to eliminate as many as possible without any member losing a sense of choice, that is, never sacrifice consensus.

○○ Once elimination is decided on, facilitator draws a single line through the dropped candidate numbers (and their first round count) on the matrix sheet.

○○○ Asks someone to cross out equalivent numbers on the wall-hung text flip chart sheets.

○○○ Calls out numbers being crossed out to ensure no errors and that everyone knows what numbers to cross out on their personal count sheets.

○ Round two of voting begins with facilitator telling members to review candidates and choose a maximum of half of them for the second round of voting.

○○ Count total remaining, declare one-half number.

○○ Give sufficient time for members to think privately on choices (obviously depends on number remaining).

  ○○ Remind members not to exceed maximum number of allowed votes.
  ○○ Round 2 votes are called, counted, and recorded using same procedures as in first round.
   ○○○ Vote count entered in third column of matrix sheet (next empty column to the right of round 1 column).
 ○ Procedure continues through elimination rounds as defined above.
  ○○ Ends under one of the following conditions:
   ○○○ Final choice (or choices) completed.
    ○○○○ Occurs when members decide that they are satisfied with final surviving candidate(s).
   ○○○ Surviving candidates are few enough to finish voting using either convergent NGT or discrete summation and members decide to use one of these techniques.

1.2.5.2 Nominal Group Technique (NGT)

Features

Convergent NGT is a private technique for ranking or prioritizing statement candidate finalists. I have found that it works best when approximately 20 candidate statements remain to be considered. Members seem to be able to juggle that many ideas with relative ease, but NGT becomes visibly more difficult when the number of candidates gets larger.

  The results of voting are not significantly changed by the choice of technique to be used during the finalist rounds. I have tested this proposition numerous times and feel quite confident with the results. Considering that the same people are looking at the same candidates, under the same conditions, there is little reason to expect a difference in finalist selections.

  The most positive remarks that I hear about convergent NGT are that it gives participants a quiet time to think and allows then to cast private ballots. However, as I mentioned earlier, teams often agree to switch techniques during successive divergence/convergence episodes just for the sake of variety. Regardless of the technique used, during the finalist rounds of voting, each individual is privately prioritizing or ranking surviving candidates in his or her own mind. The different techniques are, in effect, merely different ways of summing and expressing these singular private decisions. The decisions remain quite constant, regardless of the technique chosen to express them.

  The NGT process is mechanically easy. Each member is given a number of 3 by 5 inch cards and asked to format them to record two distinct numbers. With approximately 20 remaining candidates, I usually distribute five cards per person. If there are 12 or fewer remaining candidates, then I distribute four cards per person. Members are asked to select five (assuming five cards were distributed) candidate statement finalists from out of the survivors. They are then asked to write the statement number of each of the five finalists on the cards, *one number per card*, in a designated format area. Using what has sometimes been called an overly ritualistic (but I believe necessary) ceremony, each member is then asked to rank his or her five finalists with respect to each other. The *most favored* of the the five finalists selected by each individual is to be given a *weight score* of "5" on the card (in another designated format area) bearing that candidate's statement number (the "5" score signifying the most favored finalist for that individual). From the four remaining cards, individuals are asked to select the *least favored* candidate and give it a score of "1" in the appropriate formatted area. This most favored, least favored sequence is repeated (with scores of "4" and "2") and the last remaining card is given the median score of "3."

The most–least device reflects the fact that it is easier to choose extremes than it is to choose between median preferences. With this technique, the median choices are identified by default. It works with any number of choices and cards.

When voting is completed, the cards are collected and sorted, first by individual statement numbers and then by weights for each statement. The necessity for the ritualistic procedure required during voting becomes obvious at this juncture. If card formats vary and numbers are illegible, inconsistent or intelligible, the entire ranking process is jeopardized. And once the cards are mixed, it just about always proves impossible for individuals to recognize their own cards or to reconstruct their exact thought processes. Clarity and precision are vital.

The weights for each statement receiving them are recorded by the facilitator underneath the appropriate statement text on the wall-hung flip charts. The top finalist is the one receiving the highest cumulative weight. If two or more statements score the same weight, then the tie is broken by counting the total number of cards (reflecting the total number of individuals who chose that candidate as a finalist) submitted for each of the candidates. A tie is declared between any two or more statements that receive both equal weights and equal numbers of votes.

I have found convergent NGT very helpful when the mechanics of multivoting, carried down to final selections, fails to reflect a true sense of consensus in the room. In fact, any one of the three finalist techniques described here make fine consensus assurance devices when one of the other two leaves an atmosphere of dissatisfaction hovering in the air.

Procedures (Figures 6-11, 6-12)

○ Facilitator distributes cards (five for example) to members.
  ○○ Give following instructions:
    ○○○ Lay cards out in pattern (Figure 6-11A).
    ○○○ Make no marks or entries on cards until instructed. *Please observe this restriction* (explain reason).

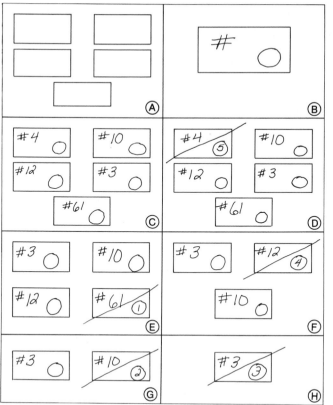

Figure 6-11 Convergent NGT Voting Procedure

ooo Format each card with "#" symbol in center and large circle in bottom right corner. Use dark pencil or pen and be neat (Figure 6-11B).

ooo Each member please consider the remaining semifinalist candidates and select your five finalists (give them ample time).

ooo Enter one finalist statement number on each card, next to the "#" symbol, neatly and clearly (Figure 6-11C).

ooo Do not . . . repeat . . . do not proceed further and please do not move ahead of my pace.

o Individual members follow the instructions and stop after each of their five cards contains the formats and the numbers of their chosen statement finalists.

o Facilitator gives following instructions:

oo We are now going to weight ("1" to "5") our finalists with respect to each other. A weight of "5" is to be given to the *most preferred* finalist and a weight of "1" is to be given to the *least preferred* finalist; intermediate weights are to be distributed in descending order of preference.

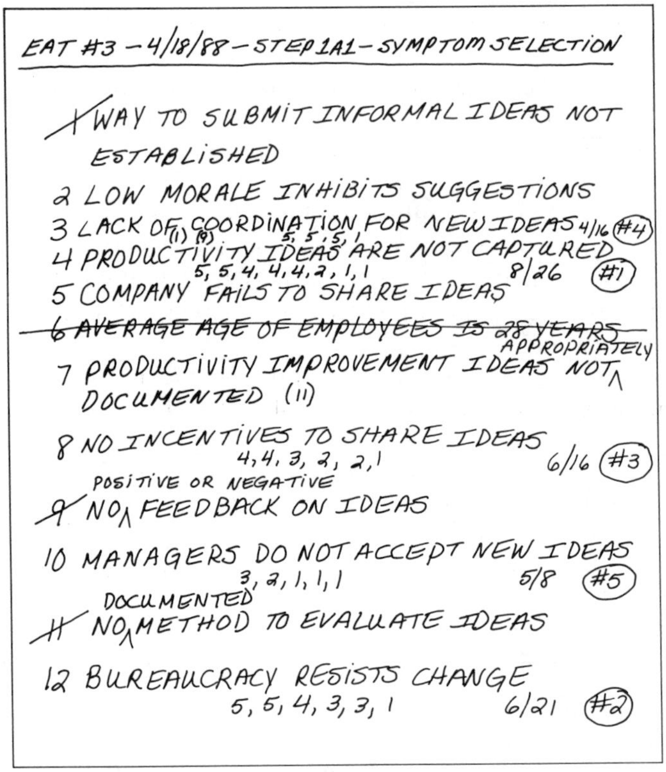

EAT #3 – 4/18/88 – STEP 1A1 – SYMPTOM SELECTION

X WAY TO SUBMIT INFORMAL IDEAS NOT ESTABLISHED

2 LOW MORALE INHIBITS SUGGESTIONS

3 LACK OF COORDINATION FOR NEW IDEAS 4/16 (#4)
(1) (9)   5, 5, 5, 1

4 PRODUCTIVITY IDEAS ARE NOT CAPTURED
5, 5, 4, 4, 4, 2, 1, 1   8/26   (#1)

5 COMPANY FAILS TO SHARE IDEAS

6 AVERAGE AGE OF EMPLOYEES IS 28 YEARS

7 PRODUCTIVITY IMPROVEMENT IDEAS NOT APPROPRIATELY DOCUMENTED (11)

8 NO INCENTIVES TO SHARE IDEAS
4, 4, 3, 2, 2, 1   6/16 (#3)

POSITIVE OR NEGATIVE
9 NO FEEDBACK ON IDEAS

10 MANAGERS DO NOT ACCEPT NEW IDEAS
3, 2, 1, 1, 1   5/8 (#5)

DOCUMENTED
11 NO METHOD TO EVALUATE IDEAS

12 BUREAUCRACY RESISTS CHANGE
5, 5, 4, 3, 3, 1   6/21   (#2)

Figure 6-12 Typical Flip Chart Sheet: Convergence NGT

○○ *Repeat! Please do not enter weights now . . . follow my pace.*

○○ First, select your most preferred finalist, enter a weight score of "5" in the bottom right circle, turn the card over, and *Stop* (Figure 6-11D).

○○ Second, you now have four finalist cards. Select your least preferred of the four finalists, enter a weight score of "1" in the bottom right circle, turn the card, over and *Stop* (Figure 6-11E).

○○ Third, you now have three finalist cards. Select your most preferred of the three finalists, enter a weight score of "4" in the bottom right circle, turn the card over, and *Stop* (Figure 6-11F).

○○ Fourth, you now have two finalist cards. Select your least preferred of the two finalists, enter a weight score of "2" in the bottom right circle, turn the card over, and *Stop* (Figure 6-11G).

○○ Fifth, you now have one finalist card. Enter a weight score of "3" in the bottom right circle, collect all five of your cards, and pass them to the facilitator (Figure 6-11H).

○ Declare a 5 to 10 minute coffee break and ask two members to assist with the card sorting procedure.

○○ Sort the cards by statement number and lay the piles out on the table in sequential statement number order.

○○ Sort each pile by weight values, "5's" on top, "1's" on bottom, in descending order of weight values.
○ Facilitator writes scores for each statement underneath text on wall-hung flip chart sheets.
○○ One team member reads the weight scores aloud for each pile of cards.
○○○ Begin with the lowest statement number.
○○○ Members recite the weight scores individually, beginning with "5's" and continuing in descending order of weights through "1's", that is, "Statement number 17: 5, 5, 4, 4, 4, 3, 2, and 2."
○○○ Facilitator writes the weights under text for statement number 17, exactly as recited.
○○○ Total the number of cards for statement number 17, that is "8".
○○○ Add the sum total of the weights: $5 + 5 + 4 + 4 + 4 + 3 + 2 + 2 = 29$.
○○○ Write the two totals (number of scores/total weight) under the statement text on the far right side of the flip chart sheet that is, "8/29."
○○○ Read the scores for statement 17 as follows: "Statement 17 received 8 votes for a total weight of 29; that is, 8 for 29."
○○○ Repeat process for every pile of sorted cards.
○ Seek the statement on flip chart sheets with the highest total weight score and declare that as the consensus preference.
○○ Repeat the process for second, third, and so on, highest weight score.
○○ Rank statements with equal weight scores according to number of votes received.
○○ Declare statements with both scores equal as *tied* in rank.
○○ Note that the number of statements receiving high finalist scores does not necessarily equal five (because five cards were distributed to each member).
○○ Total number of high scoring finalists depends on distribution of individual member choices during the card writing process.
○○ Note aloud that rather large score differences separate the cluster of big winners from the median and small winners. This top-scoring cluster is usually the group to concentrate on as the team moves on to the next PIC step and the next set of techniques.

1.2.5.3 Discrete Summation

Features

I coined the title "discrete summation" for this convergent technique. However, the device, itself, is hardly original. I have seen it described in a number of documents, always with some variation of form or structure. My experience indicates that, like convergent NGT, psychological barriers reduce the usefulness of discrete summation as the number of statements to be ranked grows beyond a certain number. I suggest that it is best employed with no more than 10 to 12 statements. For simplicity's sake, I shall explain it under the assumption that there are 6 finalist statement numbers to rank. The principle is as easily learned with this number as it would be with 10 to 12 statements.

The term discrete refers to choices between two distinct, separate, clearly distinguishable alternatives. This is exactly the task given to each individual member of the team during the first part of the technique. Each member privately ranks each alternative against each of the other alternatives in a kind of round-robin contest. Therefore, each comparison pits one candidate finalist against one other candidate finalist, for example, 1 versus 2, 1 versus 3, . . . , 2 versus 3, 2 versus 4, . . . , 3 versus 4, 3 versus 5, . . . , 4 versus 5, 4 versus 6, 5 versus 6. Each specific contest is between one of two distinct alternatives, and the choice of one alternative is taken at the cost of the other. Mechanically, the winning choice is simply circled in each binary contest on a specially prepared form.

The second individual task is to add (sum) the number of times each of the finalist candidates (six in the enclosed example) wins a discrete contest. This is easily done on the special form by simply counting the number of times each candidate's number is circled. With six alternatives, there are a total of 15 discrete round-robin contests. With five alternatives there would be 10 contests, and with seven alternatives there would be 21 contests. Therefore, a parity check of the total number of votes made by each person against the total number of available choices can be easily made.

When everyone has completed their private voting, the forms are collected, and the total votes for each of the six finalists are tallied (summed) on the special team form. A parity check is also available on this second form. If, for instance, five team members (as assumed in the example) are involved, then the total number of available team votes is 75: (15 votes per person) × (five people).

Each person can also check the logic or his or her discrete choices. Logical inconsistencies can occur in the process. For instance, a person could choose candidate "X" over candidate "Y," and candidate "Y" over candidate "Z," but, at the same time choose candidate "Z" over candidate "X." Such inconsistencies become relatively easy to discover as the device becomes more familiar with repetition. As a final ranking tool, discrete summation is probably best constructed to illuminate such inconsistent thinking. Regardless, it is simply one more mechanical tool to help individuals calculate and present their principal ideas and conclusions.

No doubt, other techniques are available to conduct convergence voting, and I encourage everyone to seek them out and use them to their best effect. Just be careful to examine the strengths, weaknesses, and limits of each such device and be sure that it is being employed for the right reasons, with respect to the particular PIC phase/stage/step under current investigation.

Procedures (Figures 6-13, 6-14)

○ Facilitator distributes discrete summation individual voting forms, one per member, and explains voting process.
  ○○ Enter statement numbers of finalists to be ranked.

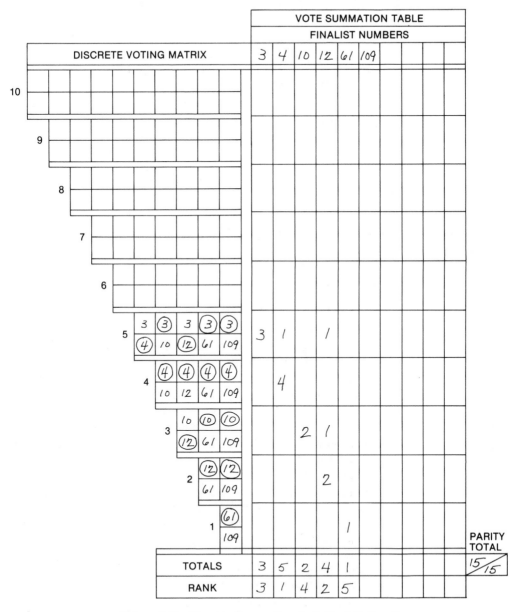

Figure 6-13 Discrete Summation: Individual Voting Form

TEAM MEMBER	FINALIST CANDIDATES										PARITY
	2	3	4	7	8	10	12	34	61	109	
1		3	5			2	4		1		15
2		1	4			3	4	1			13
3		2	5	1	1	1	3		2		15
4		3	5			2	4			1	15
5	1	2	4			1	5		1		14
TOTALS	1	11	23	1	1	9	20	1	4	1	72 / 75
FINAL RANKING	6	3	1	6	6	4	2	6	5	6	

Figure 6-14 Discrete Summation: Team Voting Form

○○○ Assume that the six finalist statements used in this example are "3, 4, 10, 12, 61, 109."

○○○ Order the numbers low to high.

○○○ Enter the numbers in the heading squares of the *vote summation table* section of the individual voting form (Figure 6-13).

○○○ Enter the number "15" in the bottom right segment of the *parity total* square (15 discrete votes with six candidates).

○○○ Note that the *Discrete Voting Matrix* section of the form is constructed of ten numbered discrete comparison levels, each level divided into two rows and a number of column squares.

○○○ Each of the six finalist statement numbers can be individually contested five times, that is, once for each of its five competitors.

○○○ Find level "5" in the matrix and enter the candidate numbers as shown in Figure 6-13.

○○ Conduct individual discrete voting.

○○○ Begin at level "5."

○○○ Decide your preference for number "3" versus "4."

○○○ Circle the winning number.

            ○○○ Repeat the process for the remaining four comparisons in level "5."

            ○○○ Repeat the process in levels "4" through "1."

            ○○○ If you are totally indifferent about the two alternatives in any discrete contest, that is, your preference for one is exactly equal to your preference for the other, then *circle neither of them.*

        ○○ Sum the votes for each candidate finalist.

            ○○○ Add the number of circles around each number in level "5."

            ○○○ Enter totals in the appropriate columns of the summation table (Figure 6-13).

            ○○○ Repeat the process for the remaining levels.

            ○○○ Add the entries for each candidate in the appropriate columns of the summation table.

            ○○○ Enter totals at the bottom of the summation table.

        ○○ Conduct the parity check.

            ○○○ Note that the parity number (the maximum number of available votes with six alternatives) is "15."

            ○○○ Add the total number of votes cast and enter in the upper-left segment of the *Parity Total* square.

            ○○○ Ensure that the total is less than, or equal to the parity number (indifference votes reduce the total).

            ○○○ If the total votes cast number more than the parity total, review the entries on the form and correct the error(s).

    ○ Facilitator collects forms.

    ○ Team selects two members to enter individual voting totals on *Discrete Summation Team Voting Form*, as shown in Figure 6-14 (assuming five team members in this example).

        ○○ Enter parity check totals, as required, for individuals and for team.

            ○○○ Enter the number "75" in the bottom-right segment of the parity total square (15 votes/person $\times$ 15 people).

            ○○○ Ensure that the sum of individual parity totals is less than or equal to, "75."

            ○○○ If the total votes cast number more than "75," then review all forms and correct the error(s).

            ○○○ Enter final ranking numbers in the bottom row of the form.

                ○○○○ Finalist with the highest vote total is ranked "1," that with the lowest total vote is ranked lowest.

Convergence/Divergence Summary

Many pages have been devoted to explaining the detailed mechanics of D/C. A newcomer to the PIC might infer that any device requiring so many pages of explanation must be complex, difficult to learn, intricate, and user unfriendly. However, the opposite is true. During my typical four-hour and one-day PIC orientation workshops, people who have never heard of such processes exercise D/C with sufficient skill to use it the next day in their own organizations. One complaint that I hear from people attending some quality improvement seminars and schools is that instructions for conducting suggested processes are not provided in sufficient detail to actually exercise. Well, D/C, as explained here, is one of those exact tools for bringing the principles of quality improvement to sparkling life. Of course, you can best learn the technique by participating in an orientation workshop or team. But, failing that, you can construct the event with the blueprint provided above. In Chapter 7, you will find vignettes that humanize the PIC and put some flesh on the bones rattled in this chapter.

But I want you to understand that if you start participative decision making, motivation enhancement, morale boosting, personnel empowerment and communications improvement with nothing more than a D/C experiment, you will come away with a solid feeling of accomplishment and a renewed faith that you can beat back the devils plaguing your corporate halls.

If you try D/C without a trained facilitator, you will stumble. But just remember Shuster's law about failure and fear of failure: it is all part of learning. By all means, I recommend that you hire a trained facilitator. It will be one of the best investments you ever made. But, if that is impossible, distribute some copies of this book, read and discuss D/C (within the context of the previous chapters), and give it a try. Properly executed, the D/C experiment will be so successful, liberating and uplifting that the motivation for probing deeper into quality management practices will be firmly enough established in enough individuals to rethink a few priorities.

The remainder of the techniques (see Table 6-1) detailed in this chapter are often used in conjunction with D/C (see Figure 6-2), but they are sufficient unto themselves and merit close investigation on their own merits.

2. STREAM ANALYSIS

Features

Remember that PIC Stage 1A, *Symptom Selection*, is a three-step process for speculating about a symptom of interest, verifying the speculations, and finally specifying an exact symptom statement. Stage 1A, then, is the anchor for any PIC exercise, because it is the reference point against which causes and resolutions for a symptom are compared and evaluated. It is meaningless to seek causes and resolutions for a symptom until the symptom, itself, is clearly identified.

Stream Analysis is a technique for logically defining symptom statements by separating them from other kinds of expressed statements, for example, cause, resolution, or impact. It is used, therefore, during PIC Steps 1A1 and 1A3, both before and after symptom verification.

Remember that symptom statements must be expressed in terms suggesting no direct causes or solutions, for example, "I have a stomach ache," as opposed to "My ulcer is giving me a stomach ache." The most important early decision to be made in any issue resolving situation is to determine the *condition of interest* that the symptom statement is to express. For instance, is the ulcer the condition of interest, or is it the stomach ache? Or is it, perhaps, the impact of it all, for example, that I cannot go to work with the pain? Clearly, a logical reference point must be established against which the symptom can be expressed, its causes can be identified, and potential impacts, or results, can be estimated. Like motion, all such standards are relative. For instance, how fast is a jetliner flying? Is its speed to be measured with respect to the velocity of the air streaking across its wings (airspeed)? Or is it to be fixed with respect to a stake driven into the ground (ground speed)?

How should we measure the length of a room, by inches, meters, centimeters, cubits, miles, parsecs, feet? And what is a "foot?" How do we *know* that any given strip of imprinted wood represents a *true* foot? What if two different rulers are different in length by a factor of $\frac{1}{16}$ of an inch? Which of the two sticks represents the true foot? Are they both off the mark? What is the standard? The answer is that the standard is *conventional*; that is, it is not ingrained in an absolute law of nature. Conventional standards are contrived by human beings, defined for convenience and accepted by consensus. In the case of conventional rulers, they can be calibrated for accuracy by comparing them to a standard rod that is probably encased in a temperature controlled atmosphere somewhere in the tombs of the Bureau of Standards. That rod represents the standard foot, by consensus. Therefore, the term accuracy is meaningless when applied to rulers until the *standard foot* is defined. So it is also in stating the speed of an aircraft; it must wait upon the standard of evaluation (airspeed or ground speed).

Think of symptom definition as equivalent to "driving a standard reference stake into the ground," against which all related elements can be gauged. It is equivalent to driving that stake into the ground as a reference against which to measure the groundspeed of the jetliner.

The title Stream Analysis suggests the flow of *cause and effect*, for example, the ulcer *causes* the stomach ache (*effect*), which itself causes absence from work (*impact*), as illustrated in Figure 6-15(a). If we wish to investigate this stream of events, our first step is to focus on the element that best expresses the condition giving rise to our interest. If we decide that absence from work is our proper focus, then we must express it in terms that do not suggest specific causes, that is, as a symptom. An example symptom might be, "Average weekly absence rate is 22 percent of employee population." This is now our symptom, stated as an effect. Clearly, stomach aches are only one of many potential causes for this effect. Reduced productivity is one potential impact of absence.

However, if we decide to focus on the stomach ache, then the symptom

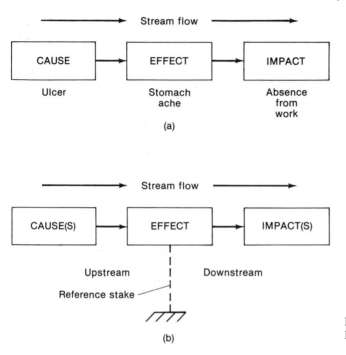

Stream flow

| CAUSE | EFFECT | IMPACT |

Ulcer   Stomach   Absence
               ache   from
                                work

(a)

Stream flow

| CAUSE(S) | EFFECT | IMPACT(S) |

Upstream   Downstream

Reference stake

(b)

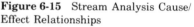

Figure 6-15 Stream Analysis Cause/
Effect Relationships

(effect) might be stated as, "Employees are reporting increasing incidences of stomach aches." Absence then becomes an intermediate impact, with productivity losses representing an even further end impact.

Maybe an increasing incidence of ulcers is the focus of interest. The ulcers, then, are treated as the symptom (effect), with potential causes including stress, drinking, and so on. One intermediate impact could be stomach aches, with further ramifications of absence and lowered productivity.

The point of all this is that the most critical mental threshold to cross in selecting a symptom statement, is to establish the location in the flowing stream of cause and effect where the reference stake is to be driven and against which all other elements are to be evaluated. Figure 6-15(b) illustrates this concept. The *symptom* (effect) is defined as that element in the cause/effect stream determined to be the staked reference point against which all other elements are defined. Clearly, with respect to the direction of cause/effect flow, all causes are upstream of the symptom and all impacts are downstream of the symptom.

Frankly, I have found this Stream Analysis concept to be the most abstract in my current arsenal of techniques. It is the one that newcomers to PIC find most tricky to use. But it is essential. An issue must be defined before it can be resolved. The key to comfort rests in understanding that the approximate condition (issue) of interest must be clarified before stake driving is considered. All sorts of daily pressures constrain us from taking the time to think through such basic questions. The initial question to ask is, "What is the condition in the working environment that caught our attention in the first place?" This condition (or issue of interest) becomes the effect, that is, the location of the stake. The next step is to state that effect as a symptom. Cause and impact statements are relatively easy to isolate once these basics are determined.

Procedures (Figure 6-16)

○ Obtain a general working consensus regarding the general issue of interest.
　○○ Does not have to be exact.
○ Identify those statements written on the flip chart sheets that are:
　○○ *Symptoms*, or statements that:
　　○○○ Directly express the issue of interest (effect).
　　○○○ Do not imply a direct, tangible solution.
　　○○○ Do not imply a cause.

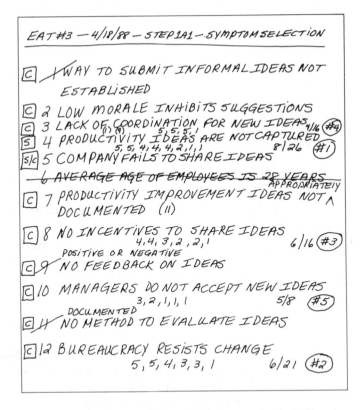

Figure 6-16 Typical Flip Chart Sheet: Stream Analysis Notations

- ○○ *Causes,* or statements that:
  - ○○○ Create or account for the symptom.
  - ○○○ Imply resolutions.
  - ○○○ Are located upstream of the symptom.
- ○○ *Impacts,* or statements that:
  - ○○○ Result from (or are caused by) the symptom.
  - ○○○ Imply consequences of the symptom.
  - ○○○ Are located downstream of the symptom.
- ○○ *Resolutions,* or Statements that:
  - ○○○ Suggest recommendations for action.
  - ○○○ Imply some improvement in the symptom.
- ○○ *Facts,* or Statements that:
  - ○○○ Verify symptoms, causes, impacts, and resolutions.
  - ○○○ Are stated in precise numbers, for example:
    - ○○○○ "The average loaded labor rate is $24.59/hour."
    - ○○○○ "Eighty percent of respondents declared that they do not share their ideas with other people."
- ○ Label statements near the left margin, as follows (Figure 6-16):
  - ○○ Symptoms:
    - ○○○ "S"
  - ○○ Causes:
    - ○○○ "C"
  - ○○ Impacts:
    - ○○○ "I"
  - ○○ Resolutions:
    - ○○○ "R"
  - ○○ Facts:
    - ○○○ "F"
  - ○○ If a statement appears to fit into more than one category, label it accordingly (statement "5," Figure 6-16).
    - ○○○ Statement "4" is the only entry unambiguously labeled "S."
- ○ Actual case history (Figure 6-16).
  - ○○ Team convened to consider following general condition of interest:
    - ○○○ "Employees often develop better ways to do their own jobs, but no one else ever seems to hear about them."
    - ○○○ Total of 32 statements generated during Step 1A1, 12 of which appear in the figure.
      - ○○○○ Stream analysis identified three statements as symptoms, labeled "S."
      - ○○○○ Four statements identified as facts, labeled "F."
      - ○○○○ Remainder identified as causes, labeled "C."
    - ○○○ Final converged Step 1A1 statement was:
      - ○○○○ "Company fails to capture individuals' productivity improvement ideas."

○○○ Verification (Step 1A2) and further refinement (Step 1A3) confirmed statement with no changes.

3. CAUSE/EFFECT (C/E) DIAGRAMMING (FISHBONE/ISHIKAWA)

3.1 Factors Types

Features

Dr. Kauro Ishikawa (1976) developed the "fishbone" diagram to assist analysts to logically identify, sort out, and categorize all the potential causes for a specified effect (symptom). Recall that he defines quality as "nondispersion of quality characteristics" (Table 2-1). He wondered why, at the output of a manufacturing process, individual items of the same product differed in some quality characteristic. For example, why do the diameters (quality characteristic) of ball bearings differ (dispersion) as they come off of the assembly line? Or why does the roundness (quality characteristic) differ (dispersion) between individual bearings? He wanted to isolate all the potential factors (causes) that might account for such dispersions. Factors might include temperature variations and pressure changes in machines or actions taken by employees. They might also include features of raw materials or elements of the total manufacturing process, itself.

Ishikawa was interested in ensuring clarity of thinking and focused concentration during the causation discovery process. He was also interested in simplicity of display and ease of comprehension. As Figure 6-17(a) illustrates, the familiar outline of a fish, including the internal skeletal structure, enjoys all these virtues. It also conveys a sense of flow and direction. One's eye naturally moves left-to-right across the page; tail-to-head toward some implied end or destination. These virtues are retained in the abstracted illustration of the fishbone [Figure 6-17(b)]. The tendency to "look to the right" culminates in the head block.

What we are calling a symptom (effect) is written in the block. Each rib bone becomes the main trunk of a general category of potential causes. Ishikawa refers to a symptom as a quality characteristic and to causes as factors. Therefore, using the ball bearing example, the symptom might be stated as "Ball bearing diameters vary from the specified length by ±15 percent" (Figure 6-18). Team members are free to determine the appropriate causation categories for any given diagram. An example is shown in the figure, where four categories (ribs) are defined, *Press Machine, Environment, Process*, and *Employees*, one rib per category.

Divergence is used to generate as many statements of causation as possible. It is vital that team members focus on the symptom at all times. The fishbone format makes that quite easy, since the eye is easily drawn to the

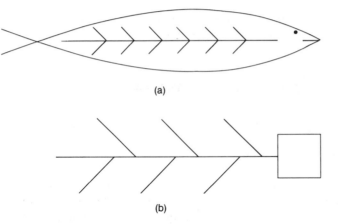

Figure 6-17 Derivation of Ishikawa "Fishbone" Cause and Effect Diagram

symptom statement written in the head box. During a typical divergent brainstorming session, one member suggested that the statement "temperature variation" be entered under the *Press Machine* category. This started people thinking, and sometime later in the exercise someone suggested that one cause for the temperature variations could be "poor temperature monitoring," leading to the subsequent suggestion that an underlying cause could be "insufficient metering."

The number of fishbone entries is limited only by the knowledge, expertise, imagination, and patience of the team members. Of course, the sheet can get very crowded very quickly. I always tape a 2 by 2 collection of four flip chart sheets together when beginning this kind of *factors* Ishikawa diagram. Attention to spacing and clarity of printing also helps. Additional sheets can always be added. Another way to approach the crowding is to tie all entries directly to the main rib of each category. The gain in neatness and crowding is offset, however, by a loss of the logical linkages between general causes and their root subcauses. These linkages can subsequently be defined by using the *WHY–BECAUSE Pursuit* technique described later in this chapter.

One of the most pervasive myths surviving to this day is that this technique is useful only for manufacturing issues. Perhaps it is related to Ishikawa's original manufacturing focus of interest. Forget it! Purge this imagined limitation from your mind! If the exercise is to link causes to effects, then this technique works . . . regardless of market type.

One interesting twist on the factors type diagram is the "4M's" categorized version. It can become very bothersome to try to identify major factor categories up front or to keep adding them during the divergence process. The way around this is to define four categories that cover all factors common to all production processes, manufacturing, and service. These universal *factors of production* are defined in basic management and economics courses and should be familiar to students as Land, Labor, Capital, and Management/ Entrepreneurship.

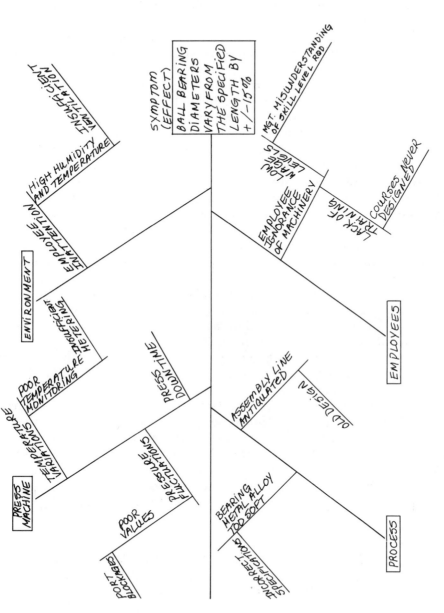

Figure 6-18 Sample "Factors" Type Fishbone Diagram

SYMPTOM
(EFFECT)

BALL BEARING
DIAMETERS
VARY FROM
THE SPECIFIED
LENGTH BY
+/-15%

HIGH HUMIDITY
AND TEMPERATURE

INSUFFICIENT
VENTILATION

EMPLOYEE
INATTENTION

ENVIRONMENT

POOR
TEMPERATURE
MONITORING

INSUFFICIENT
METERING

PRESS TIME
DOWNTIME

TEMPERATURE
VARIATIONS

PRESS
MACHINE

PRESSURE
FLUCTUATIONS

POOR
VALVES

PORT
BLOCKAGES

ASSEMBLY LINE
ANTIQUATED

OLD DESIGN

BEARING
METAL ALLOY
TOO SOFT

INCORRECT
SPECIFICATIONS

PROCESS

MGT. MISUNDERSTANDING
OF SKILL LEVEL REQ.

LOW
WAGE
LEVELS

EMPLOYEE
IGNORANCE
OF MACHINERY

LACK OF
TRAINING

COURSES NEVER
DESIGNED

EMPLOYEES

The 4M's equivalents are *Material, Manpower, Machinery* and *Methods*. All causes pertaining to the symptom will fit within one or more of these four categories. A 4M's factors type fishbone diagram requires, therefore, only four ribs, thereby simplifying and universalizing the format. Individual causes are entered into a category according to the suggesting member's best guess. They are rearranged by category only at the end of divergence/convergence (as described earlier), when all entries have been thoroughly thought out and ranked in importance. Table 6-3 defines the 4M's in terms of the sources of causes that contribute to a specified symptom (effect).

During the initial divergence exercise, it is most important to get potential causal statements onto the sheets. Therefore, the suggestor's initial guess is good enough and the scribe should enter the statement wherever the member chooses. Remember, divergent exercises such as brainstorming and NGT are not to be interrupted for any reason, including categorizing. To get used to the 4M's terminology, consider under which category some of the ball bearing statements in Figure 6-18 might best be entered. For instance, any entry that can be traced to inherent faults in the capital equipment, such as the press machine, would be entered under *Machinery*, that is, capital equipment. Possible candidates are "press downtime" and "poor valves." Causes traceable to inherent flaws in the raw materials would be entered under *Materials*, for example, "bearing metal alloy too soft." Entries such as "low wage levels," "lack of training," and "courses never designed" are rooted in management decisions and would be properly entered under *Methods*. A possible *Manpower* candidate is "employee inattention." Sometimes the true category is not so obvious at first. For instance, "press downtime" could ultimately be traced more to poor maintenance and inspection than to an inherent flaw in the press machine itself. Or it might be traced to both factors, thereby justifying its entry under *Machinery, Methods,* and *Manpower*, suggesting inherent machine failure, poor maintenance decisions, and worker apathy and inattention. Such meanings become more obvious as the Divergence/Convergence process develops. The object, of course, is to diverge as many possible causes as possible and then converge down to the one or few causes deemed most critical. Assuming that the appropriate people are on the team (as defined in Chapter 7), the chances

TABLE 6-3 Definitions of Cause/Effect Diagram 4M's Categories

Category	Source or Cause
Manpower	*Individual* behavior and attitudes
Methods	The *way* things are done; for example, rules, procedures, resource allocations, specifications, standards, instructions, organization, management
Machinery	What people *work with*; for example, facilities, resources
Material	What people *work on*; for example, raw materials and information received to be further processed, inputs

are very good that the highest ranked causes will be verified during the next PIC Step (1B2). Once the few finalists are chosen, the team can develop a consensus about categorizing each of them. If all the finalists concentrate in one of the 4M categories, then that says a lot about the character of the possible resolutions. If, for instance, they all collect under *Methods*, then resolutions will be aimed at the organization, decision-making process, and procedures. A totally different perspective would develop if the causes collect under *Machinery*. This event would suggest taking a very careful look at facilities and capital equipment. If the critical causes spread throughout the 4M's, then potential resolutions would have to cover a much broader range of actions.

The finalist causes derived by the team investigating the capturing and sharing of productivity ideas provide an illustration of how they can congregate in one or two 4M categories. Over 80 statements were generated on the fishbone during divergence. They were reduced to the few critical causes shown in Figure 6-19. Note that the critical causes are almost evenly divided between *Methods* (organization) and *Manpower* (individual attitudes/behavior). Two entries (numbers 17 and 78) are included in both categories, indicating a belief that both organization and attitudes are at the heart of these causes.

Some of these critical causes are stated in such broad terms that they do not suggest tangible and precise resolutions. The WHY–BECAUSE Pursuit, described later in this chapter, is a technique used to clarify the *root*, or subcauses for broadly stated surface causes. The ultimate object is to isolate precisely stated critical causes of the symptom. Once they are verified and ranked according to degree of contribution to the symptom, members are well on their way to forming resolution ideas in their minds.

Procedures

○ Tape four flip chart sheets together in a 2 by 2 pattern and hang horizontally on the wall.
○ Draw the fishbone design on the sheet.
  ○○ Write the symptom statement in the head box.
  ○○ Write the word "Symptom" above the box.
○ Conduct divergence exercise.
  ○○ Ask members to state two things when offering an entry:
    ○○○ The 4M category into which the statement is to be included.
    ○○○ The statement, itself.
○ Conduct convergence exercise.
  ○○ During CDAM, do not be concerned with the fact that combining statements will sometimes require moving them across categories. Go ahead and move them. Their initial placement is merely suggestive.
  ○○ After finalists have been voted, sketch a small version of the fishbone diagram in the corner of the large sheet and enter just the numbers of

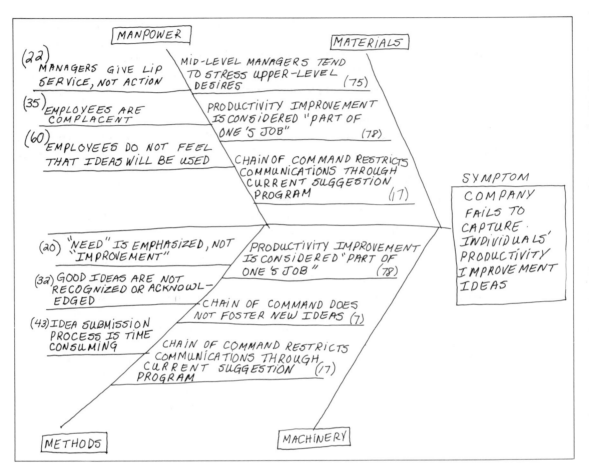

Figure 6-19 Convergent Fishbone Diagram

the finalists into the categories that team members select (by consensus).

∞ Take a few moments to consider the distribution pattern and its implications for potential resolutions, for example, the implications if all the finalists are concentrated in one or two categories or if they are spread evenly throughout all of them.

3.2 Process Type

Features

Another type of Ishikawa cause/effect diagram is the *Process Type*. It is very useful when investigating the potential causes of a symptom occurring in an operation where the individual sequential steps in the process are clearly defined. Imagine, for instance, the step-by-step procedures for publishing a technical bulletin. Figure 6-20 illustrates an example of a very broadly defined publishing process. Assume that the symptom being investigated is "The average actual processing time, from step 1 through step 7, is 2.5 times longer than the allocated time." What are the potential causes? The diagram allows members to focus on potential causes occurring in each of the specific steps. Figure 6-21 is a simplified reproduction of Figure 6-20. The lines extending from each process-step box are equivalent to the rib lines of the 4M's fishbone diagram. Again, I recommend that the full process diagram be drawn on four (or more) taped flip chart sheets, including full labeling of each step. During divergence, members state the box number and the cause. The scribe writes the cause statement on the appropriate rib, as illustrated in the figure.

The standard convergence technique is conducted (numbering through voting), and the critical causes are isolated similarly to the factors-type operation. Process-type fishbone diagrams can be as general or as detailed as the team desires. I have facilitated teams that stretch a process across the entire length of a 30-foot wall. Standard flow charting symbols, including decision (yes/no) diamonds, can be used to break down a process to its minutest details. Every flow diagram box is labeled with a number, an action identification, and responsible job categories. One of the most surprising discoveries that team members make, as they develop detailed process flow diagrams, is the complexity and richness of the steps that have to be completed in order to accomplish what was thought to be a rather simple operation. The number of required feedback loops is also surprising. My experience shows that this particular technique is enlightening and very fruitful. It takes time and patience, but results in very clear and tangible causes.

Procedure

- ○ Tape a number of flip chart sheets together and hang horizontally on the wall.
- ○ Conduct members through flow chart development to level of desired complexity.
- ○ Redraw final chart, distributing boxes at distances most conducive to extending fishbone ribs.
  - ○○ If possible, format diagram to stagger adjacent ribs above and below the line of flow.
- ○ Conduct members through a typical Divergence/Convergence exercise.

4. WHY–BECAUSE PURSUIT

Features

WHY–BECAUSE is an extension of the Ishikawa concept. I personally find it most useful as a device for extracting the deep root subcauses of individual fishbone finalists. The technique could be used directly against the symptom

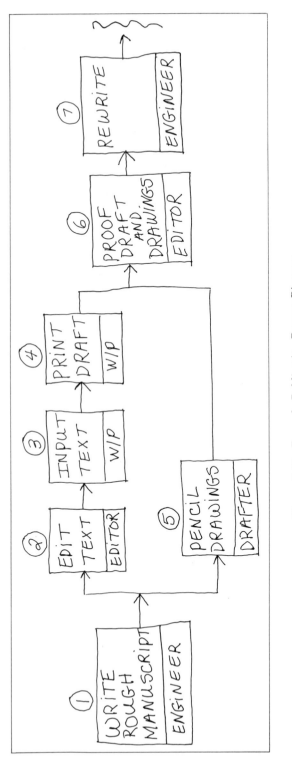

Figure 6-20 Example Publication Process Diagram

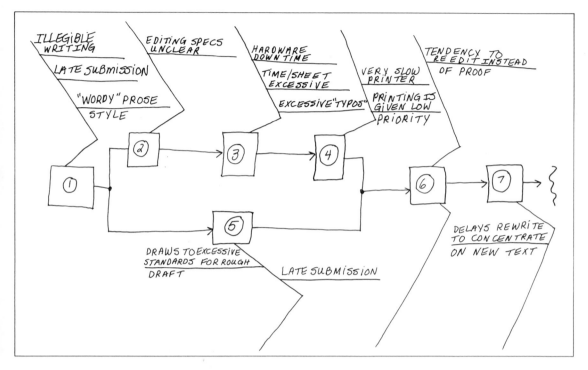

Figure 6-21 Example Process Fishbone Diagram

statement, and I do not doubt that some people use it just that way. But I suggest otherwise. The reason is that the Ishikawa technique is entirely open and freewheeling in its rules for divergence. Any entry is acceptable for inclusion in any category. The object is to generate as many causal possibilities as imagination and knowledge allow.

WHY–BECAUSE is more restrictive. The term pursuit is an apt descriptor of the technique. Designed in the form of a logic tree, the technique requires that entries bear a logical linkage to one or more previous entries. The object is to pursue the logical origin of a more broadly stated cause down to its fundamental roots. This is why I prefer to use the fishbone technique first. It allows totally open consideration of possible symptom causes, whereas WHY–BECAUSE plunges one's mind into the depths of a single cause's genesis.

Figure 6-22 illustrates the logic of WHY–BECAUSE. The initial cause statement is written in the box. During a divergent brainstorming exercise, the first suggestor states the cause and then asks, "Why?" He or she then answers "Because," followed by the actual answer. The scribe writes the answer on the first available branch, for example, branch A. The scribe does not write the word "because" for each statement. It is implied for every statement. However, I do recommend that the prefix statements "Why?" and "Because" be au-

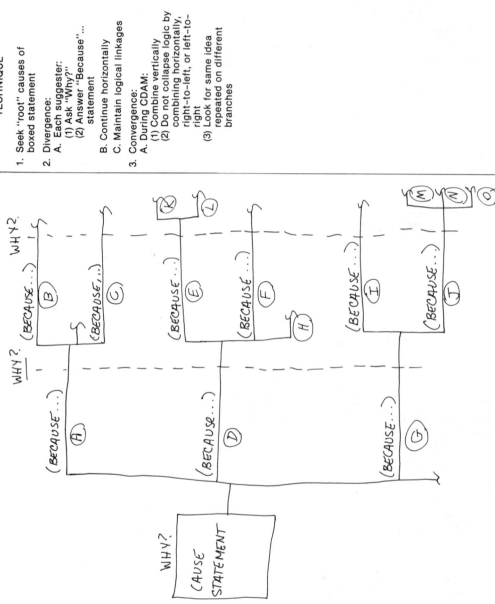

TECHNIQUE

1. Seek "root" causes of boxed statement
2. Divergence:
   A. Each suggester:
      (1) Ask "Why?"
      (2) Answer "Because"... statement
   B. Continue horizontally
   C. Maintain logical linkages
3. Convergence:
   A. During CDAM:
      (1) Combine vertically
      (2) Do not collapse logic by combining horizontally, right-to-left, or left-to-right
      (3) Look for same idea repeated on different branches

Figure 6-22 Why-Because Pursuit Logic and Format

dibly uttered, at least until people become very familiar with the pace and flow of the logical requirements for linking each statement to its predecessor.

The logic flows in the following manner (Figure 6-22):

- "D" causes the original boxed statement.
- "E," "F," and "H" cause "D".
- "K," and "L" cause "E".

The most logical way to read the cause/effect relationship, however, is to stay on one horizontal path at a time, as follows:

- "K" causes "E".
- "E" causes "D".
- "D" causes original cause.

To give this pattern more substance, consider the ball bearing fishbone diagram illustrated in Figure 6-18. Note the cause listed under the Employees category: "Employees ignorance of machinery." There are two subcause branches attached. Note how, in Figure 6-23, these subcauses can be extended further and further down into their root origins. Follow one line of reasoning:

- Employee ignorance of machinery . . . Why?
  - Because . . . of . . . lack of training . . . Why?
  - Because . . . it was . . . never considered necessary . . . Why?
  - Because . . . we . . . never did it before . . . Why?
  - Because . . . managers did not want training . . . Why?
  - Because . . . it is . . . time consuming . . . Why?
  - Because . . . .

The numbers are not added to the diagram until divergence is completed. Remember that item numbering is the first step in convergence. A few more main branches of reasoning can be added to the diagram. However, I caution teams to beware of too many main branches. The object is to think *horizontally*, that is, to get at the roots of the few main streams of causation. If more than four or five main lines of reasoning develop (vertically), then there is reason to suspect that members are free-thinking the same universe of causes stated on the fishbone diagram; that is, they might be merely re-creating the fishbone in a different format. Some of the statements will certainly appear on both diagrams, but the rationale for including them in the WHY–BECAUSE Pursuit should be logical linkage. This process of linking statements logically is sometimes called *entailment*.

The WHY–BECAUSE Pursuit technique is often cited as the favorite by newcomers to the PIC. The reason is that it leads to conclusions that are totally nonobvious at the start, and yet are so logically valid. It is not at all uncommon for 100 to 200 statements to be entered during divergence.

The rules of convergence are few, but vital:

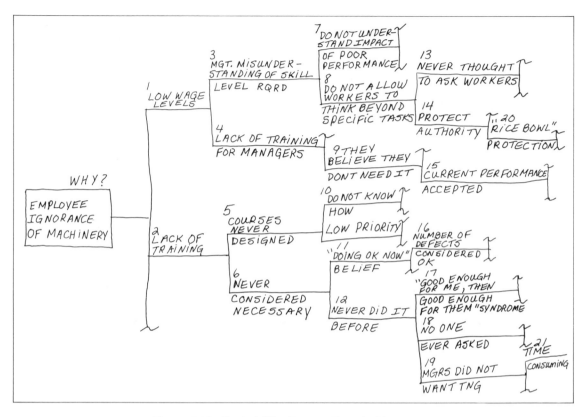

Figure 6-23 Typical Why-Because Pursuit Diagram

○ Number top-to-bottom, left-to-right (Figure 6-23).

○ During CDAM, combine vertically, not horizontally. Some people fall into the trap of collapsing horizontal lines of reasoning, for example, combining "16" under "11," then "16/11" under "6," then "16/11/6" under "2." This not only defeats the purpose of the technique, but it violates the rule of combining, which says "do not combine statements because one is the cause of the other." Statements should be combined only if they so closely restate each other that to vote for one would be tantamount to voting for the other. It simplifies voting by removing the need for redundant votes. Try to combine similar statements that appear in different branches. One possible combination in Figure 6-23 would be "16" under "15," or "15" under "16."

○ When combining two entries, all attached statements do not move with the subordinate statement. For instance, if item "12" is combined under another statement, items "17 to 21" do not move with it. WHY–BECAUSE, like its partner techniques, is merely a device to stimulate creative thinking and consensus. Once a causal statement is written in any logical path, it stands alone on its own merit and can be isolated or moved as its criticality requires. The statements attached to it are helpful in generating more entries and become very useful as analytical tools for reasoning through solutions in PIC steps 2A1 to 2A3. Statement independence is a keystone of this technique.

Team members decide exactly how many WHY–BECAUSE Pursuits to conduct for any given assignment. I recommend that the universe be restricted to the number of fishbone diagram finalists. And there is no reason to assume that all the finalists must be put through the WHY–BECAUSE Pursuit. The critical determinant is the shared sense that the team has isolated the fundamental root causes of the symptom. If that can be done with several fishbone finalists and one or two WHY–BECAUSE Pursuits (one each for one of the fishbone finalists), then that is sufficient. My experience indicates that conducting two WHY–BECAUSE Pursuits sharpens everyone's insights so clearly regarding the root causes of the symptoms that people seldom see a need to go further. But I have always seen the need for at least one WHY–BECAUSE Pursuit.

Procedures

- ○ Tape sheets (2 by 2 sheets minimum) and hang horizontally on wall.
- ○ Draw box at left center and write in the fishbone finalist being analyzed.
- ○ Write "Why?" above the box.
- ○ Extend a short horizontal line to the right from the box and then extend a vertical line, as shown in Figure 6-23.
- ○ Conduct divergence using structured brainstorming.
    - ○○ Ask each member to state two things during a turn:
        - ○○○ On which branch the statement is to be attached.
        - ○○○ The statement itself.
        - ○○○ A typical entry (Figure 6-23) would be stated: "Off of 'Lack of Training for Managers,' Why?; Because . . . 'They believe they don't need it.' "
    - ○○ Add sheets as required.
    - ○○ To best anticipate crowding, add first main branch at top, second at bottom, third in middle, and so on.
- ○ Conduct Convergence as usual to isolate critical root cause finalists.

5. PROCESS INTERNALIZATION

Features

This technique is original, at least as presently constructed. Over the years, I have noted a recurring theme centering on the notion that the way things are *supposed* to be done and the way that they *are* done are often quite different.

This insight is certainly no great shock. Everyone seems to understand it. And almost everyone has experienced it. However, I began to ask what the signs might be when "supposed" and "actual" do approach each other and start to coincide. I turned, again, to the concept of process.

Assuming that a *process* is any set of sequentially arranged actions for arriving at a desired end, I asked myself why one process becomes actualized, while others are abandoned. The answer, when it came, was almost too obvious to be useful. The answer is that a process becomes *actual* (the way things really are done) when it becomes internalized within an organization. A process is *internalized* within an organization if and only if it is ingrained in the culture of the people doing the work. Again, our focus is on the individual. Again, I reiterate my concentration on the individual as the origin and source of everything that happens in any organization.

Formal and Informal Processes

We usually learn the strict and unforgiving rules of group norms and peer pressure in early school grades. Those who are most dense usually suffer hard lessons as preteens and teen-agers. We learn that, regardless of the rules, certain things *are* done and other things *are not* done. One early personal and enlightening experience with this truth, in a professional setting, occurred at the beginning of my last assignment in the Air Force. I had spent almost three years at Keesler Air Force Base, Mississippi, teaching electronics and radar systems to future maintenance technicians and officers. Everything was taught by the book, for example, how to use a technical manual, how to troubleshoot a circuit, how to read a schematic, how to fill out maintenance reports, how to conduct preventive maintenance, how to conduct test procedures. It was all formalized and neatly packaged. And I had spent three years of hard study learning and teaching the entire package. Therefore, I enjoyed a 2300-mile, first class train ride to Yaak Air Force Station, Montana, confident and secure in my knowledge of it all and certain of my value to the lucky people about to receive my services.

It is amazing how quickly we learn when survival is at stake. The Riviera-like strip of the Gulf Coast, from Mobile, Alabama, to New Orleans, Louisiana, bears little resemblance to a tiny military radar station perched atop a 5000-foot mountain peak rising a minimum of 60 miles from even the most remote village, buried in 10-foot drifts of snow and embraced by chilling −60° breezes. The mountain lion, bear, and other assorted wildlife were also a bit of a change. Sum it all up with the words *remote* and *isolated*. My attitudes changed as quickly as the geography, technically as well as behaviorally, in this setting. For instance, there was never a dispute between maintaining and troubleshooting the equipment by the book or by some informal but universally understood process. There simply was no book. In the 10 months of my tour, I do not remember ever touching a technical manual, let alone referencing one to use a procedure. Troubleshooting was some arcane ritual practiced by long-timers, that is, 15 to 20 year NCOs whose mysterious ways could have as easily been learned at the feet of a far eastern guru as in the gleaming classrooms of Keesler's Allee Hall. Ten years with the equipment taught them odd ways, and each sergeant's "ways" left when he did, only to be replaced by the equally shrouded expertise of his remaining disciples. I never did get the hang of it, but I was great at handing them tools.

I learned quickly about the difference between informal and formal processes, although I had not yet formed the concept in my mind. Informal processes are the stuff of culture. Formal processes are the children or organization. Organizations are bloodless. Culture is in human marrow and sinew. In conflicts between the two, there is no contest. Marrow and sinew overwhelm roles and rules. One of quality management's great advantages over traditional management is its real recognition of this crucial truth.

My thoughts on the application of this concept to quality improvement began to crystallize a few years ago as I heard this recurring theme in **Teaming** sessions. It occurred most often during causation analysis. Statements such as, "It'll never happen," "Yes . . . we have procedures, but they never seem to work," "The procedures are not clear," "I never saw the procedures, but everybody says the exist," and so on, became commonplace. This is when the dichotomy between *Informal Process Internalization* and *Formal Process Internalization* jelled in my mind. And I realized the potential power these concepts had for clarifying causation, and therefore solution, analyses. In terms of Stream Analysis (pages 80–85), Process Internalization statements arise during PIC causation and solution stages and are seldom characteristic of statements generated during the PIC symptom-finding stage.

Figure 6-24 identifies both formal and informal process internalization. A short period of consideration will show that a process can be informally internalized without being formally internalized. It can be both formally and informally internalized. But it cannot be formally internalized without first being informally internalized. Very simply, if it meets all four formal internalization criteria, then it must (by definition) satisfy the informal internalization criterion.

Can a process be neither formally nor informally internalized? Frankly, I think not. Somehow, whatever a process is, it gets performed. It might not get done properly, its results might always be unsatisfactory, and no one in the office might be capable of expressing how it is attempted. But unless there is absolutely *zero* action taken with respect to the process, it *is* attempted. And the *way* it is attempted is the tangible indicator of the informal internalization.

5.1 Informal Process Internalization

The definition of Informal Process Internalization in Figure 6-24 should be self-explanatory, especially in light of the discussion in the last few pages. Habits need no justification. In fact, the surest way to scare the wits out of peo-

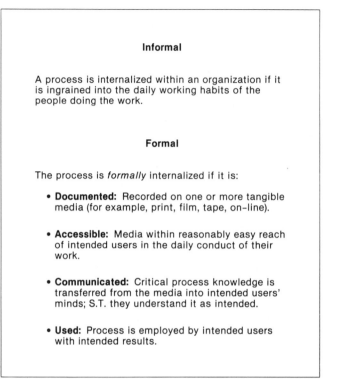

Informal

A process is internalized within an organization if it is ingrained into the daily working habits of the people doing the work.

Formal

The process is *formally* internalized if it is:

- **Documented:** Recorded on one or more tangible media (for example, print, film, tape, on-line).

- **Accessible:** Media within reasonably easy reach of intended users in the daily conduct of their work.

- **Communicated:** Critical process knowledge is transferred from the media into intended users' minds; S.T. they understand it as intended.

- **Used:** Process is employed by intended users with intended results.

Figure 6-24 Process Internalization

ple is to challenge comfortable niches, even those that often irritate us. To quote Colonel Blake in the popular TV series *M*A*S*H*, "better the devil you know." Machiavelli's insights into the human fear of change, cited in the *The Prince*, are often found excerpted on office walls. If you want to test this proposition, announce to your people that you have decided to physically rearrange the office in the near future and that you are currently deciding who will be placed where and with what facilities. Be prepared for every known sign of stress. You will probably discover some new strains that no one ever dreamed of. Habits are hard to change, but not because new habits are hard to *learn*. It is, rather, because old habits are hard to *unlearn*. This is why quality gurus say that it takes years for traditional organizations to rise when impregnated with quality yeast. The bulk of the time is spent unlearning.

You will often hear that quality management principles are common sense and obvious. Why then are they so scarce and so difficult to acquire? The answer is that we hold to our habits like a hapless soul who clings tenaciously to a twentieth-floor balcony railing as the last protection from falling into a fearful 250-foot abyss. Lectures on how we might have avoided falling off the balcony in the first place are not really high on our list of priorities as our fingers slowly slip around the cold metal.

Habits, then, are the mortar binding informal processes together.

5.2 Formal Process Internalization

When informal processes are cited as causes of problem symptoms, the reasons always seem to center around four criteria that repeatedly emerged as I thought and rethought about the phenomenon. After several iterations, these four criteria are currently worded as shown in Figure 6-24. When team members focus on processes and procedures as the culprits underlying a symptom, I suggest that they try to isolate which of the four criteria best describes the character of the cause. The technique is easy to apply. The trick is to focus on the four criteria in order, that is, "documented" first and "used" last.

A process is formally *documented* if it is tangibly recorded, as stated in Figure 6-24. The issue is not so much the *correctness* of the documentation as its *existence*. Clues to its correctness and completeness are gleaned from answers to questions about the next three criteria.

Accessible documents are easily obtained. How many times have you heard, "I'm not sure who has it," "Yeah, it's somewhere," "We can send for it . . . maybe get it in eight weeks," "It's on disk, but we can't get one," or some such other disclaimer.

Communicated has a very special meaning in this technique. It gets to the heart of understanding. Documented processes are meaningless if they are either not understood or are insufficiently understood . . . as intended by the creators of the document. Information is communicated, in this context, therefore, if (and only if) it is fully transferred from accessible documents into the minds of intended users.

Sometimes people do not use what is properly communicated to them. A documented, accessible, and communicated process is *used* (and only if) it is employed as intended by appropriate people.

A process is *Formally Internalized* if (and only if) it fully conforms to all four criteria. If it does not so conform, then the root cause can be accurately isolated by identifying which of the four criteria is *first* violated. Therefore, I recommend that this process is best introduced during the clarifying portion of cause/effect (fishbone) convergence. All of the ideas have been entered on the fishbone diagram, and members are in the correct frame of mind to reconsider what they really meant when suggesting each idea during divergence. Their minds are focused in exactly the right direction to learn and use this concept.

Procedures

- ○ Read and discuss the meaning of the terms:
  - ○○ Process
  - ○○ Informal internalization
- ○ Read and discuss the four criteria for formal internalization, in the following order:
  - ○○ Documented

    oo Accessible
    oo Communicated
    oo Used
  o Facilitator uses examples of fishbone entries to explain possible meanings, for example:
    oo "No standardized process for moving outgoing correspondence through the department."
      ooo First ask question (answer yes or no):
        oooo "Is a standardized process documented?"
      ooo If answer is yes, then ask second question (answer yes or no):
        oooo "Is the documented standardized process accessible?"
      ooo If answer is yes, then ask third question (answer yes or no):
        oooo "Is the documented and accessible standardized process communicated?"
      ooo If answer is yes, then ask fourth question (answer yes or no):
        oooo "Is the documented, accessible, and communicated standardized process used?"
      ooo If answer is yes, then there *is* a standardized process and the causal statement can be doubted.
      ooo If the answer to any one of the questions, asked in the appropriate order, is no, then the causal statement is reinforced (assuming later verification), with its root being identified as residing in that criterion for which the answer no was stated.

Further refinements of root causes can be accomplished by joining this technique to the causal statements diverged during the WHY–BECAUSE Pursuit and to solution statements diverged during the resolution stage.

6. DATA/INFORMATION ACCUMULATION

PIC Steps 1A2, 1B2, 1B3, 2B1, and 2B2 involve verification, that is, the accumulation and/or analysis of data for the purpose of testing the validity of speculations. The Divergence/Convergence steps are speculative and their outcomes must be verified empirically. However, this book is not about specific techniques for conducting empirical research, developing questionnaires, sampling populations and performing statistical analysis. Juran's books (see Bibliography) discuss some of these topics, and pertinent general literature is easily found in any academic library.

There are, however, a few related ideas about empirical analysis worth discussing at this point. They include hints about how to initiate the search for data, how to display it, how to use it to prioritize and rank conclusions, and how to recognize the difference between *information* and *data*.

6.1 Information and Data

Information is substantive knowledge conveying meaningful insights about some topic of interest. *Data* (datum is the singular term) are specific isolated bits of measurement (usually numerical) that verify the truth, falsity or degree of truth and falsity of information. For instance, suppose that a supervisor is told by a number of employees that the single computer terminal in the office is always busy and that they never seem to be able to use it when required. The information to be obtained is something like "Is the computer terminal sufficiently available to employees?" Examples of pertinent data include:

○ Number of employees
○ Number of employees who legitimately use the terminal
○ Number of terminals
○ Density of use during each hour of a typical workday
○ Specific hours of use by each employee over a period of one month
○ Specific hours of use by task over a period of one month

Examples of nonpertinent data might include:

○ Height of Mt. Everest
○ Color of employees' hair
○ Local news broadcast time
○ Number of yearly personnel evaluations completed

Suppose that an employee investigating the terminal availability issue walks into the supervisor's office one morning with the following statement: "Boss, I've got an answer." "Good," comes the hopeful reply, "let's hear it." Flashing a wide proud grin, the worker chirps "Two!" After a substantial pause, the supervisor leans forward on the desk and slowly asks, "Two . . . two . . . what?" "Just two," is the reply.

Needless to say, we are leaving our hapless boss with a substantial communication problem, as well as a probable headache. Obviously, the number "two" is meaningless unless we can associate it with some pertinent aspect of the topic. For instance, what if the employee comes into the office with the following statement: "Boss, I've discovered that we actually have two computer terminals instead of one." Now that is a pertinent datum. But it is not information in this case. The substantive information concerns the degree of availability of the computer terminal . . . now possibly two terminals . . . to employees. The specific fact that there are two, instead of one, terminals available is one element of the total data set that will convey the desired information.

Team members must realize that the act of verifying symptom and causation speculations involves this ability to determine what constitutes pertinent data, how to present it once obtained, and how to collect and analyze it.

The process works something like this:

○ Precisely state the desired information, for example, "Are computer terminals sufficiently available?"

○ List the facts (data) that will convey that information. I prefer to write factual statements as if the data are already known. For instance, instead of asking "How many people are employed in the office?" I would write the statement "There are _____ people employed in this office." Another example would be: The average minutes of terminal usage, by hour, are:

HOURS	AVERAGE MINUTES
0800–0900	_____
0900–1000	_____

And so on until closing time.

All that one has to do is collect the data and fill in the blanks. The best way to display data, is in any format that will lead most quickly and most obviously to the desired information. For instance, the final presentation of hourly use might best be a bar graph or trend line. It also might include users' names to enrich insights and convey more information.

The trick is to present the facts most succinctly and comprehensively to allow the audience (the supervisor) to visualize the information by viewing the data. And keep it simple. Do not decorate charts and graphs with gargoyles and fancy trim, like some late nineteenth-century government building. Decoration hides meaning. Free it!

6.2 Pareto Presentation

Most of us are familiar with histograms, pie charts, bar graphs, line graphs, scatter plots, tables, and equations. They are generally accepted formats for displaying information. The one data display format that might be less widely known is Pareto diagramming.

Vilfredo Pareto was a nineteenth-century economist who developed a number of principles that retain wide popularity. Quality improvement specialists have locked onto one such idea that was expanded by Juran just after World War II. The concept is generally known as the *80/20 Principle*. Pareto, looking at mid-nineteenth-century Italy, found that 80 percent of the nation's wealth was in the hands of 20 percent of the population. Unequal income distribution is certainly no surprise to most of us. But we encounter the same general ratio operating in other instances. Have you managers, for example, ever noticed that about 80 percent of your personnel problems are caused by 20 percent (or fewer) of your personnel? And how many of us have joined some organization only to find that very few of the members perform the bulk of the work?

Juran discovered that the 80/20 principle also applies to symptom–causation relationships. Essentially, he suggested that 20 percent of all the causes contributing to a given symptom account for about 80 percent of the total causation. We have already discovered that fishbone and WHY–BECAUSE techniques uncover large numbers of potential causes for a symptom. Through convergence, we reduce these potential causes to a dozen or fewer. But even these dozen do not contribute equally to the symptom. The purpose of PIC causation/verification (Step 1B2) is to empirically determine the relative degree of contribution of each speculated final cause to the symptom. The Pareto principle suggests, and my experience tends to agree, that even out of the few finalists, anywhere from two to four of them contribute the bulk of causation. Therefore, these very few causes are the ones to resolve, because that will effectively erase the symptom. Such relationships are very amenable to pie chart display. Pareto diagramming is also an excellent device for displaying this information.

Figure 6-25 illustrates a basic Pareto display in the form of a skewed histogram and a table. Assume that it illustrates the degree of contribution of the verified causes for the ball bearing diameter dispersion shown in the fishbone diagram (Figure 6-18) and WHY–BECAUSE Pursuit (Figure 6-23). Assume, also, that the proportions of causal contribution are as follows:

- ○ Critical causes:
  - ○○ Press downtime   30%
  - ○○ Temperature variations   20%
  - ○○ Low priority for employee training   15%
  - ○○ Belief that current performance is acceptable   15%
- ○ Trivial causes (all others)   20%

The histogram bars in Figure 6-25 are arranged left to right, in descending order of percent of contribution to the symptom. Therefore *press downtime*, verified as contributing 30 percent of total causation, is the first column on the left. The last column represents the combined causal contribution of all the many trivial causes, too many to individually enumerate and display. The cumulative trend line plots the sum of the causal impacts represented by the columns under its slope. For instance, *press downtime* and *temperature variations* account for a combined total of 50 percent of the symptom causes. The slope of the cumulative trend line, therefore, plots an end point of 50 percent at the indicated coordinate. The Pareto histogram clearly illustrates that the four cited causes, together, account for 80 percent of the dispersion in the ball bearing quality characteristic at the end of the production process. The many

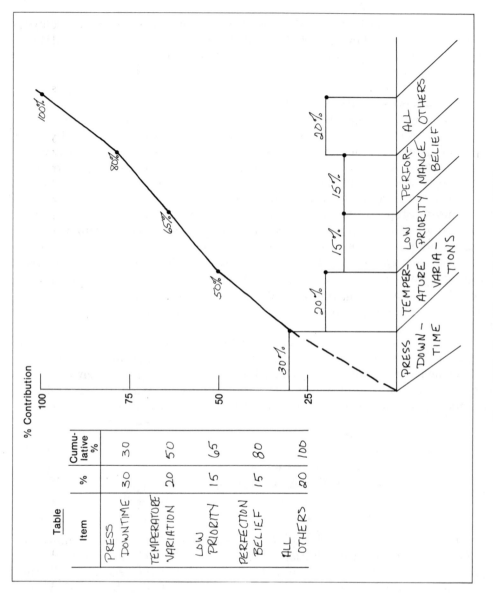

Figure 6-25 Typical Pareto Histogram and Table

"other" causes account for only 20 percent of the dispersion. The tabular format, also illustrated in Figure 6-25, is quite succinct. But I have found it to be less popular as a display format in presentations. The choice is a matter of personal preference.

One very helpful variation on the histogram format becomes possible to use after further research uncovers the potential cost of resolving each of the symptom causes. For instance, one might assume that the best approach to resolving the ball bearing symptom would be to eliminate or drastically reduce press downtime. This would effectively eliminate 30 percent of the symptom. The next cause to attack would then logically be temperature variations, thereby eliminating 20 percent of the symptom. But what about cost? Assume, for instance, that eliminating press downtime would be very expensive, but that eliminating temperature variations would be relatively very cheap. This could (and should) be a critical consideration in determining how to resolve the issue.

Figure 6-26 is a revised version of the Pareto histogram. The width of the columns represent the estimated *relative* dollar costs of solving the ball bearing dispersion by attacking each of the cited causes. Quite a different message is conveyed by this second histogram. The cost/benefit ratios suggest that attacking temperature variation and performance belief might be the most logical first steps. At relatively little cost, their resolution could account for removing 35 percent of the symptom causes, a not insignificant reduction in ball bearing dispersion. The information gleaned by displaying the data in this format is impressive. The width of any column indicates its relative cost. The height shows its relative benefit. And the slope of the cumulative trend line located directly above that column indicates its combined relative cost/benefit impact on the symptom.

The initial causation impact Pareto diagram, derived from causation data accumulated during Step 1B2, will not usually include resolution cost figures. Therefore, the diagram will look more like Figure 6-25 than Figure 6-26. Cost/benefit data are usually accumulated during the resolution implementation stage (Step 2B1). Both diagrams are important. During causal analysis, resolution costs should not enter into one's thinking. The whole point of the PIC is to prevent such inhibitions from blocking peoples' thinking about the reality of situations. A real cause of a symptom is no less real simply because its resolution might be expensive. However, when costs of resolution do become appropriate considerations, it can be very valuable to compare cost-free and a cost-encumbered Pareto diagrams. Such considerations become critical entries in Force Field Analysis, described later in this chapter.

Summary

Collecting, formatting, and analyzing data for the purpose of conveying meaningful information is often tedious and frustrating. But it is essential to any

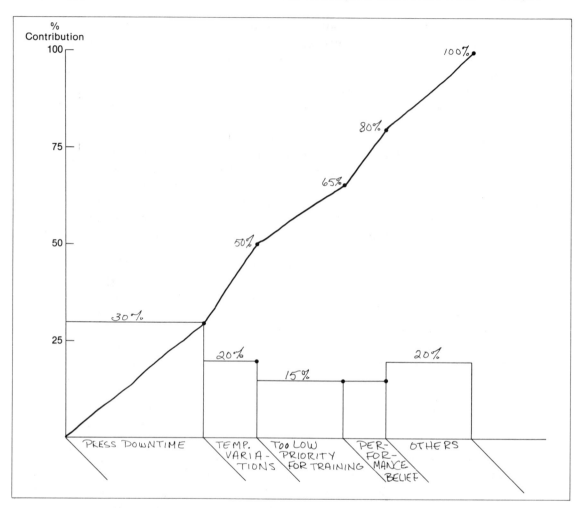

Figure 6-26   Cost/Benefit Pareto Histogram

good investigation. Resist the temptation to avoid or reduce it. Nothing can be more frustrating than to complete an entire investigation only to find that the effort was unnecessary and the results ineffective. And there are few experiences more rewarding than presenting to an audience, innovative performance improvements that shatter damaging myths of conventional wisdom with incontrovertible empirical evidence. Remember that the PIC phases and stages are divided into alternating steps of speculation and verification, each crucial to the effort and all combining to assure success.

7. HOW–BY PURSUIT

Features

Structurally, the HOW–BY Pursuit is identical to the WHY–BECAUSE Pursuit. It is a logic tree. Ideas are entered onto branches according to the dictates of logical entailment. Divergence and convergence are also employed in the same manner for both techniques. But the similarities end at that point. Functionally, the HOW–BY Pursuit is designed to discover *how* broadly stated solutions and recommendations for action are to be accomplished.

Figure 6-27 shows the format of a typical HOW–BY Pursuit logic tree. The technique for diverging ideas is, again, similar in principle to the equivalent exercise in the WHY–BECAUSE Pursuit. The first suggester reads the recommendation statement. This statement is a call to *do* something. Therefore, the member asks the question "How?," meaning how is the recommended action to be done? After asking how, the member then says "by," and makes a statement beginning with a verb.

Figure 6-28 abstracts one small corner of an immense HOW–BY Pursuit developed by the team investigating the problem that company employees were not sharing the excellent ideas that most of them developed to make their own jobs easier and more productive. The causation and verification steps led the members to six overall solutions, one of which was "Develop a Productivity Improvement Idea (PII) Sharing Plan." The completed HOW–BY Pursuit diagram covered 14 taped-together sheets and included over 200 entries. The logic tree had 12 main branches, some of which branched out to as many as 10 subtwigs.

The purpose of any HOW–BY Pursuit is to discover the critical steps required to implement the very abstract and generally stated recommendation. Along with cost/benefit analysis and consequence analysis, the exercise gets to the heart of recommendation feasibility. It is important for members to understand that the timing of implementing actions and their relative sequencing are not a concern at this time. The object is merely to isolate and define the crucial steps required to conduct the recommendation. Scheduling can be done later. Once divergence is completed, team members converge down to the relatively few statements most critical for successfully implementing the boxed solution statement. Again, the rules of convergence are the same as applied in the WHY–BECAUSE Pursuit technique. Number entries top to bottom and right to left. Combine vertically, not horizontally, for example, numbers "9" and "11." With over 200 entries spread over 12 main branches, clarification, combining, lobbying, and voting can take substantial time. But size, complexity, and time are usually measures of the complexity of the overall issue itself. The issue, by its very nature, takes care and patience. It would probably never

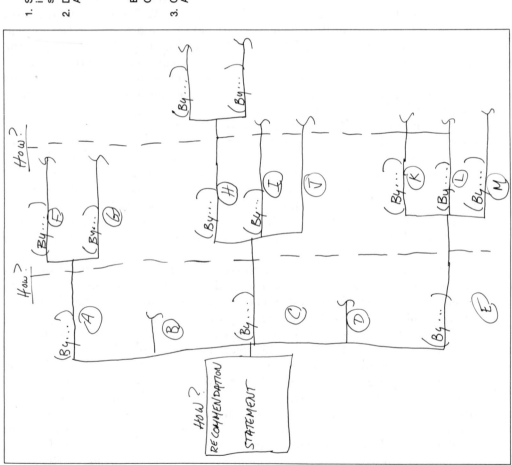

Figure 6-27 How-By Pursuit Logic and Format

110

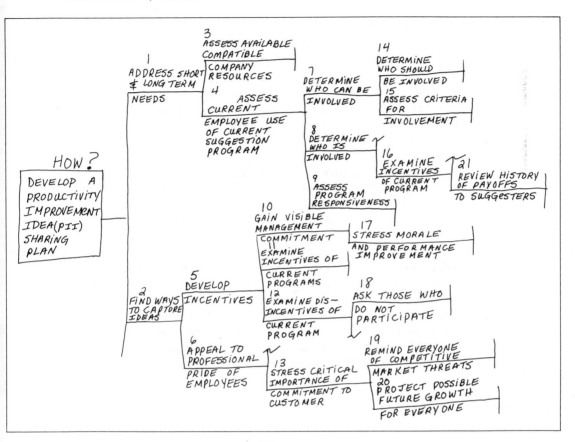

Figure 6-28 Typical How-By Pursuit Diagram

have become such a monster if equally careful attention had been paid to it earlier. It is reality staring you in the face. So face it back. Do not fall victim to impatience and cries for taking shortcuts. It is at times such as these that commitment is truly tested. The PIC will work . . . if you work. If you don't . . . it won't!

Procedures

○ Tape a minimum of four flip chart sheets together (horizontally 2 by 2) and tape them to the wall.

○ Write the solution/recommendation statement at the left-center margin and enclose it in a box.

○ Write the word "How?" above the box.

○ Draw the first vertical line of the logic tree.

○ Conduct divergence.

∞ Remember that each finalist can be treated as an independent statement and that its selection does not impose the necessity of including attached statements as finalists.

Remember that CDAM combining in logic trees such as WHY–BECAUSE and HOW–BY pursuits should be done vertically (across branches), not horizontally (within and along branches). Also remember that these techniques are designed to stimulate creative thinking that identifies critically important insights.

It is important to realize that every statement in a logic tree is *independent*. Therefore, when a statement is moved for combining, its adjacent, logically related branch statements do not move with it. And when a statement is chosen as a finalist, all the statements in its branch of reasoning are not chosen with it.

However, the full line of statements, within which a finalist is logically embedded, provides very helpful hints regarding how to implement that idea. For instance, both the WHY–BECAUSE and HOW–BY finalist entries and their logical interdependencies would prove very helpful during consequence analysis (force field diagramming) and cost/benefit analysis. The particular example extracted here was crucial to the people who eventually wrote the PII sharing plan. This plan is now successfully implemented and has accounted for substantial performance improvements.

8. FORCE FIELD ANALYSIS

Features

Force Field Analysis is a technique for generating, displaying, and analyzing the *consequences* of a solution/recommendation. The HOW–BY Pursuit tells us *how* to do something. Force Field Analysis tells us *what* could happen because we did it. Typical force field diagrams divide suggested consequences of actions into the two following possible categories:

○ Driving forces
○ Restraining forces

Driving forces encourage (drive) us to implement the solution; that is, they are good, positive, or pro consequences. Restraining forces discourage (restrain) us from implementing the solution, that is, they are bad, negative, or con consequences. We have all heard of "cures" that are worse than the illness they are designed to eradicate. Resolution feasibility is, in part, a function of consequences.

A separate force field diagram is developed for each solution recom-

WT	DRIVING FORCES	RESTRAINING FORCES	WT
3	LARGE # OF IDEAS WILL BE CAPTURED	RESISTANCE TO CHANGE	1
3	PROFESSIONAL IMPORTANCE WILL BE RECOGNIZED	MORE WORK FOR DEPT'S	2
		COST TO IMPLEMENT	2
3	POTENTIAL LARGE $ SAVINGS	MGT. RESISTANCE TO ALLOCATING RQ'D TIME	2
2	SOME PEOPLE WILL FEEL MORE IMPORTANT IN PROGRAM	HARD TO SUSTAIN IN LONG RUN	3
3	POTENTIAL MORALE IMPROVEMENT	PAST HISTORY OF SIMILAR PROGRAMS NOT ENCOURAGING	3
2	INCREASED AWARENESS OF PROCESS	RESOURCES / PEOPLE MUST BE USED TO IMPLEMENT	3
2	DIV. VISIBILITY IN CORPORATE	"RICE BOWL" SYNDROME DISCOURAGES SHARING IDEAS	1
2	ENCOURAGES PARTICIPATION		
1	INCREASES TOP LEVEL MGT. AWARENESS		
3	STIMULATES PII THINKING		

Within the box at top:

EAT #3 – 5/12/88 – STEP 2A2 – CONSEQ. SPECULATION

SOLUTION #52 : CAMPAIGN PII WITH THE SAME LEVEL OF EFFORT AND ENTHUSIASM AS THE ANNUAL UNITED FUND DRIVE

Figure 6-29 Typical Force Field Diagram

mended by a team. Figure 6-29 is a force field diagram suggesting the possible consequences of implementing one of the six solutions recommended by the PII sharing team. Statements are entered using typical divergence techniques. Members should be most careful to define all the possible restraining forces.

Restraining forces can only be eliminated or minimized if they are admitted and clarified. You can be sure that the audience to whom the team's final conclusions are presented will probe such considerations. And they will convey substantial credibility to team members who openly recognize and account for such considerations. Those who either cannot or will not admit, account for, and answer restraining forces are soon visualized as having done an incomplete job or as trying to hide consequences to sell an idea. Those who openly confront restraining forces and even suggest compensating factors gain immeasurable respect and attention. The bottom line is that real long-term resolutions require honest appraisal of restraining forces. Restraining forces often stimulate members to think of driving forces that mitigate or even eliminate their negative consequences. They also suggest ideas that can be added to a HOW–BY Pursuit to compensate for negative consequences. Restraining forces can often be turned into opportunities that were earlier unrecognized.

The solution for which the example in Figure 6-29 is drawn is "Campaign PII with the same level of effort and enthusiasm as the annual United Fund Drive." The numbers in the Wt columns are merely rough indicators of the strength of each entry, in terms of impact of consequence, that is, how much the entry matters. I prefer the following very general estimates of impact:

1 = Small
2 = Medium
3 = Large

These are ordinal indicators and they cannot be added to some meaningful total. The number 1 is nothing more than a shorthand indicator for the word small. Its counterparts play the same role. Therefore, you can no more add them than you can the words they represent. However, if most of the driving forces in a given force field diagram are 2's and 3's and the restraining forces are 1's and 2's, then a sense develops that the overall consequences of a solution are reasonably good. They give one an overview of the relative impact of consequences and should be treated as no more than estimates. Some people use arrows pointing into the center line to indicate weights. Three arrow lengths are used to indicate small through large impacts. Other people ignore weights entirely on the premise that they are so vague that they might be misleading. I prefer the system shown in Figure 6-29. After all, who are the team members going to mislead . . . themselves? Any device that helps convey and illustrate the sense of the team consensus is good in my estimation. This is just one more small consideration for the team to ponder. As a facilitator, I always go with the team consensus on issues that do not impair the foundations of the PIC itself or its techniques.

Statements are entered onto the diagram through typical divergent exercises. Since the object of consequence analysis is to retain all entries, there is no need to converge down to the most critical few. I usually encourage members to perform convergence through CDAM. This ensures clarification and provides an opportunity to simplify the final draft by combining or modifying like entries. Some teams number the entries; others do not.

Procedures

○ Draw the force field format on a single flip chart sheet.
   ○○ Enter the complete solution statement in the box at the top of the sheet.
      ○○○ Include the number of the solution statement as recorded on the solutions sheets during PIC step 2A1.
○ Derive the statements using typical divergence techniques.
   ○○ Ensure that members provide three bits of information for each entry:
      ○○○ The *vector* of the statement, that is, either driving force or restraining force.
      ○○○ The statement itself.
      ○○○ The estimated weight (impact) of the consequence statement.
○ Clarify and simplify the entries using typical convergence techniques through CDAM.
○ Obtain a *satisficing* consensus regarding the weight of each entry.
   ○○ A rough estimate is all that is required.
   ○○ Begin by asking the statement author his or her reasons for suggesting the original weight estimate.
   ○○ Do not belabor the issue.
   ○○ Remember to concentrate on what is agreed on, rather than what is disagreed on, when consensus is lagging.
○ Conduct a complete force field exercise for each solution finalist derived during step 2A1.
○ Hang all completed force field diagrams on the wall and cross-compare their consequences.
   ○○ Take a 15-minute working break to allow each member to evaluate consequences.
      ○○○ Look for common driving and restraining forces.
      ○○○ Isolate specific consequences that might "kill" or "guarantee" one or more solutions.
      ○○○ Find driving forces in one solution that might eliminate or minimize restraining forces in another solution.
      ○○○ Seek and record additional entries to all diagrams.
      ○○○ Consider possible modifications to existing HOW–BY Pursuits suggested by the consequence analyses.
         ○○○○ Suggest additional implementing elements that might support driving forces and compensate for restraining forces.

⚬⚬ Conduct a review of possible changes based on study.

⚬⚬⚬ Employ the rules of CDAM.

⚬⚬⚬⚬ Do *not* allow the review to degenerate into standard discussion/argument and debates between individuals.

⚬⚬ Obtain a consensus on the best estimated mix of solution finalists based on consequence analysis.

⚬ Obtain a consensus on desirability of updating existing HOW–BY Pursuits based on consequence analysis.

9. PSYCHIC IRRELEVANCY

Features

How many times have you found yourself so caught up in a situation that you could no longer think clearly about it? You needed some distance . . . some rest . . . a new perspective. And, having gained that distance, how many times did that new idea you craved just pop into your head when your thoughts were "a million miles away," that is, when you were thinking about something entirely removed from the troublesome topic? Your brainstorm was no accident. It was (what I call) Psychic Irrelevancy at play.

This technique is, by no means, original. I have seen literally dozens of variations on the theme played out in different group (and individual) decision-making enterprises. I do believe that my title is original. I like titles to convey some sense of what is occurring during an activity. I use the term psychic, because this technique emphasizes the employment of *all* our senses, imagination and insight to create ideas at *any and all* levels of consciousness. It energizes all our potential cognitive and affective resources. The term irrelevancy pertains to the purposeful intent of seeking insights about one topic by allowing our psyches to drift off into contemplation about totally unrelated and seemingly irrelevant topics.

To illustrate the process, assume that members of the team are investigating ways to increase the capturing and sharing of ideas that will improve overall work performance. We are conducting Solution Speculation Step (2A1). And we are stuck. A number of solutions have been diverged and we have even converged to some finalists. But we do not have a "warm fuzzy feeling" about our progress. That one really striking solution we all seek is alluding us. We have reviewed our causes until we are blue in the face. We feel good about them. We are just "dried out."

We could adjourn. Sometimes that works. It will certainly give us distance. But that is simply *passive adaptation* to our stress. We want *positive adaptation* (see Chapter 7 and Appendix II). Let us act to regenerate ourselves rather than quit and hope for the best. Someone suggests trying Psychic Irrelevancy. We agree. *Psychic Irrelevancy* is a technique for drawing out of our consciousness ideas that are pertinent to one topic by seeking them in topics that are, at first glance, seemingly irrelevant.

The first step in the technique is to choose one or more of our senses to use as a vehicle to stimulate our consciousness. Should we, for instance, use our visual sense, or our auditory or nasal, sense? Assume that team consensus says to use our visual sense by drawing pictures. Each person, then, is asked to sketch a picture of something on a sheet of paper and hand it in to the scribe, who hangs them side by side on the wall. The team then decides, always by consensus, which single picture or group of pictures is to be used in the exercise. Understand that there are no limits on this choice of pictures. One, a few, or all of them can be used. Understand, also, that there are no restraints on the character of the pictures. They can be as simple or as complex as imagination and time allow. Figure 6-30 includes a sample of pictures. The circled picture is the one that was chosen for the exercise. Everyone immediately recognized it, and the jokes began to fly around the room.

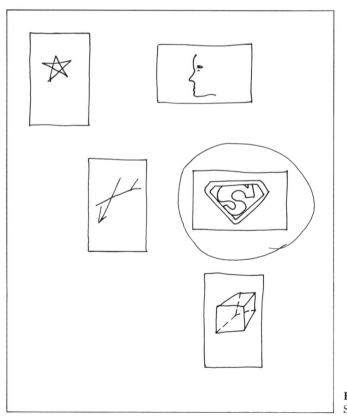

Figure 6-30 Psychic Irrelevancy
Sample Drawings

Now, at first glance, Superman's crest is about as far removed from a creative solution about capturing and sharing productivity ideas as one could get. It is, so to speak, irrelevant. But maybe a second, third, or fourth glance offers commonalties between the topics. What we are really searching for are *attributes*, at the next higher level of abstraction, that are held in common by the act of sharing and the man of steel.

The technique is quite easy to practice. The scribe stands ready to write ideas on a flip chart sheet. Members look at the picture and let their minds drift. Using random brainstorming rules, members call out whatever ideas enter their heads and the scribe records them as fast as he or she can. All sorts of ideas are forthcoming; some tangible and obvious, others less so. Possible examples include strong, alien, Clark Kent, Krypton, Lois, hero, flying, bulletproof, brilliant, virtuous, truth, justice, the American way, newspaperman, loyalty, bad guys, time travel, identity, secrets, make believe, comics, wonderful, lonely, different, homesick, inferior, winning, and on . . . and on.

Suppose that ideas such as lonely, loyalty, and identity strike a chord somewhere in the corner of your mind. You begin to associate these attributes with certain individuals recognized around the company as kind of different, out of the in-crowd mainstream. You begin to see that one of the things that makes them different is their tendency to make lots of suggestions, that is, they have a reputation of always trying to rock the boat and poke their noses in where they do not belong. But they learned! Peer pressure quieted them and now they remain alone and isolated. Suddenly you realize that they are not the only people who have learned to be quiet. You, yourself, have developed some very effective ways to better perform and you find that it would give you a nice feeling to share them with others. From that point on it is only a matter of moments before you suggest a rather surprising solution involving a cultural change, that is, reteaching people to understand that new ideas are welcome and that some boats ought to be rocked. You now know that the odd balls are not so odd after all. They possess, indeed, virtues that all of us would be proud of emulate.

You will find yourself filling with new insights and in competition with your peers to get numerous new-found solutions recorded. Psychic Irrelevancy is a kick starter and a pump primer.

The exercise could just as easily have been initiated with recorded music, or by smelling a flower, or by touching certain fabrics and surfaces. The sense stimulating vehicle can be anything that our imaginations allow. As it is with the PIC, itself, our only real limitations are self-imposed. As a facilitator, I inhibit the process only to the extent that the technique rules, once defined, are not violated. Within those rules, anything goes. Along with Wolcott Gibbs, I accept any action as valid, within the rules, as long as it is not "immoral, illegal, or fattening."

Perhaps the next logically related technique for generating ideas would be meditation. Having practiced it, I believe that there are good reasons to recommend it. But that can await further considerations.

Procedures

- ○ Stimulate a sense in one of the following ways:
    - ○○ Each member draw a picture on a sheet of paper.
        - ○○○ Scribe hang pictures on the wall.
        - ○○○ Team decide which picture(s) to use.
        - ○○○ Members look at picture(s) for a few moments.
    - ○○ Select music or some other locally convenient sound.
    - ○○ Members listen to music or sound for a few moments.
    - ○○ Pass a flower or some other locally convenient nasal stimulant around the room.
        - ○○○ Members smell the stimulant for a few moments.
    - ○○ Pass some material around the room for people to touch.
        - ○○○ Members touch the stimulant for a few moments.
    - ○○ Pass some food around the room for people to taste.
        - ○○○ Members concentrate on the stimulant taste for a few moments.
        - ○○○ Imagine, for instance, the taste of a sugar doughnut.
- ○ After a few moments of real or imagined sensory stimulation, begin a random brainstorm and record attribute ideas suggested by the stimulant on a flip chart sheet.
- ○ When brainstorm is completed, look for attributes that encourage associations with the original topic of consideration.
    - ○○ Develop the associations and record new ideas pertaining to the original topic on appropriate flip chart sheets.
    - ○○ Continue according to the rules of divergence

SUMMARY

The techniques discussed in this rather lengthy chapter represent the mechanics of the PIC. In Chapter 5, the principles and logic of the phases, stages, and steps of the process (conducted by using the techniques as tools) were defined. There are two subjects yet to cover. First, a few words should be said about what really goes on in typical **Teaming** rooms, that is, about practical attempts to use it all. Actually, it works fairly smoothly. But there are always a few little events that can add uncertainty and flavor to the enterprise. It all comes down to practice. The PIC is unbelievably user friendly. It appeals to our common sense and intuition. And aside from learning standard rules for empirical research and data gathering, which many members already understand, the techniques are absorbed almost without members realizing the effort.

The second topic for final discussion relates to certain behavioral science theories concerning why processes such as PIC are so effective. The value of the discussion is based on my belief that the best way to use something to its fullest extent is to understand its underlying principles. Simple rote memorization of formal steps robs us of the ability to think creatively, to innovate and to know the limits of the process, that is, when to break the rules to achieve the real ends. I suggest that the secret to any organization's survival is its ability to positively adapt to stressful situations through the use of feedback mechanisms. In line with Shuster's Law #2, organizations do not adapt and survive . . . people do. Adaptability is a human characteristic. But organizations, as conglomerates of people, survive based on the willingness and ability of its constituent people to collectively adapt. Appendix II offers a detailed treatment of the systems theory underlying my adaptation–survival hypothesis. It is not necessary for readers to totally immerse themselves in the complexities of the topic. But, for those who enjoy paddling up winding rivers, the appendix offers them the journey. A short review of the principles is provided in Chapter 7.

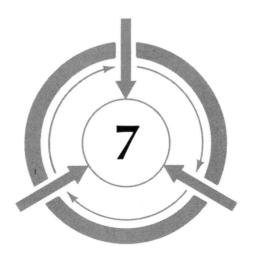

COMING TOGETHER

A man is the origin of his action.

Aristotle

Be swift to hear, slow to speak, slow to wrath.

The General Epistle of James 1:19–20

A soft answer turneth away wrath.

Proverbs 15:1

Let the counsel of thine own heart stand.

Ecclesiasticus 37:13

WHAT REALLY HAPPENS IN A TEAMING ROOM

Kinds of Teams

To understand what happens in a typical **Teaming** room, it is necessary to understand the different kinds of teams that typically exist in a mature quality environment. Table 7-1 lists my current categories of team types. This list is a product of evolution and it will continue to evolve.

The focus of this book is on Quality Action Teams (QAT). Full discussions of the Executive Council (EC), Drive Teams (DT), and Training Teams (TT) are topics reserved for a future book. However, a few short words about the interrelatedness of these various agencies are in order at this time.

The EC is the only permanent team. It has a relatively fixed membership, including the CEO, executive offices, and sometimes one or more union representatives and first-level, nonsupervisory rotating members. They do what any effective executive panel does, that is, examine and formulate the organization's corporate strategy. Their primary EC duty is to develop and maintain a prioritized list of broad issues facing the organization. They should avoid getting into specifics. Examples of issues include long-range planning, customer relations, competitive positioning, internal communications, and transportation.

Each broad issue is assigned to a DT (Figure 7-1). One member of the EC becomes the leader of one DT. Each DT leader is responsible for recruiting DT members. However, one critical responsibility of the EC is to advise each DT leader about specific DT membership. The DT remains in force as long as required, that is, until the broad issue area that gave it birth is fully resolved. It is important to understand that DT members should be drawn from across the organization. Typical horizontal and vertical barriers to communication and joint action *must . . . I say must . . .* be overcome in this recruiting effort. The criteria for choosing any team's members are discussed later in this chapter.

Each DT is responsible for isolating and prioritizing specific and tangible problem and opportunity topics within its assigned broad issue area. For instance, the internal communications DT might Diverge/Converge dozens of specific pertinent topics, including lack of coordination between accounting and production opportunities for rationalizing memoranda distribution lists.

Both the EC and DTs can use any or all of the PIC processes and techniques, as deemed appropriate. Together, they reduce broad issues of interest into specific action items. And the linkages of EC membership and DT leadership ensure that networking is maximized. Lines of responsibility and authority are evident, accepted, and supported. Direct, positive, visible, and continuous involvement of executive and top management in this **Teaming** matrix provides clear evidence of commitment and promises increasing motivation for full participation of all personnel. Nothing stirs positive feelings in workers more than unmistakable evidence that managers and executives are willing

TABLE 7-1 Quality Improvement Team (QIT) Types

○ Executive council (EC)
○ Drive team (DT)
○ Quality action teams (QAT)
    ○○ Assigned
        ○○○ Instant action team (IAT)
        ○○○ Extended action team (EAT)
        ○○○ Q-force
    ○○ Voluntary
        ○○○ Local (quality circles)
        ○○○ Regional
○ Training teams (TT)
    ○○ Orientation sessions
    ○○ Workshops
    ○○ Facilitator training

and able to work in partnership on issues of critical importance. Quality of work life leaps ahead and all sorts of symptomatic, seemingly insurmountable, stumbling blocks disappear. Again, I must reiterate that this is no panacea. It takes hard work, diplomacy, and mutual empathy. But the process does lead the way and the rewards are certain for those whose commitment is sustained.

Once a DT develops a list of prioritized action items, each member is assigned to lead a QAT to investigate and resolve one action item. Again, membership on each action team is a central responsibility of its parent DT, with assistance from EC peers.

Quality action teams attack the topics developed by the DTs. There are two categories of QATs, assigned and voluntary. *Assigned* QATs are composed of members who are appointed to the team just as they would be to any other

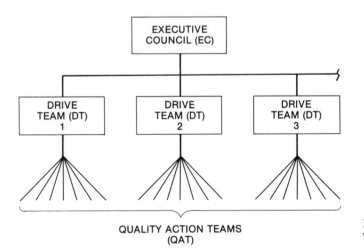

QUALITY ACTION TEAMS
(QAT)

Figure 7-1 Quality Improvement Teams Organization

task force, except that it is done through the EC/DT matrix. The issue topic each team will investigate also comes through the matrix. The team leader is an assigned member of the parent DT. When the topic is resolved, the team disbands.

Voluntary QATs are composed of members who choose, of their own free will, to join together to resolve some issue. They grow outside the matrix. However, they can be assigned DT-derived topics through negotiation. *Local* voluntary QATs are composed of people who work very closely together in a single functional work area, for example, a department secretarial pool, the machinists in a single factory location, a single building's security guards, or a department's design engineers. Their motivation is internal. There tenure is indeterminate and voluntary. These are the groups typically called Quality Circles (QC).

Regional voluntary QATs draw members from across the organization. Their interest and motivation are internally driven, but their focus is cross-functional.

Training teams convene for the purpose of learning quality management in general and the PIC in particular. Orientation sessions provide an introduction to the process, a taste, so to speak. The bulk of the time is spent in workshops, on the premise that one learns best by doing. Typical orientation sessions are scheduled from a minimum of four hours to two days.

Workshops are intense PIC training sessions. They span from three to five days. The object is to exercise both PIC phases, using all the techniques discussed in Chapter 6.

Both orientations and workshops are designed to teach the process. However, I emphasize using real issues of practical interest to participants as topics for the exercises. The real flavor of PIC is tasted best by accurately simulating a real QAT environment.

Facilitator training is critical for internalizing quality management commitment. Certain individuals display remarkable insight, talent, and interest for the PIC during training and team sessions. They must be trained by the outside professional consultant to become professionally qualified facilitators and drivers of the process. Through a process I call *bootstrapping*, they find similarly motivated peers to be trained, and they conduct orientation sessions and workshops. They also facilitate teams throughout the matrix and oversee the coordination of matrix operations. These individuals become prime candidates for the Q-Force, described later. Bootstrapping works like a chain reaction, with an ever increasing number of qualified people energizing even more people. The speed of the reaction depends on the level of commitment within the organization.

There are three kinds of assigned QATs (Table 7-1). *Instant Action Teams* (IATs) are convened to investigate short-term topics that probably will not require exercising the entire PIC. For instance, they might be asked to consider the possible consequences of a range of solutions already derived for some problem. Or they might be asked to discover the causes of a specific symptom. They might discover that the issue is broader than expected and recommend more extensive investigation. *Extended Action Teams* (EATs) look at topics requiring thorough investigation and the probable exercise of the entire PIC. The actual calendar period of their tenure depends on their schedule and various topic characteristics. Time required for data gathering is a primary determinant of all QAT tenures.

The *Q-Force* is a special agency composed of PIC-trained elites. They are on call to assist peers, operating teams, or individuals as critical needs arise.

Criteria for QAT Member Selection

Nothing is more important than selecting the appropriate people for each QAT. Selection should be regulated by one rule, vital enough to be entered as **Shuster's Law #8**:

> ALWAYS MATCH THE PEOPLE TO THE TOPIC . . .
> NEVER MATCH THE TOPIC TO THE PEOPLE

You cannot successfully ask just anyone for precise advice on just any matter. Avoid the temptation to join some people together and then give them some topic. Do it the other way. Consider the topic and then decide who could most successfully reach the best resolution. The following six criteria provide a viable guideline for QAT membership selection:

○ Interest
○ Expertise
○ Control
○ Accessibility
○ Commitment
○ Availability

Interest means that the topic should be perceived by the candidate as personally important, that is, as bearing directly on his or her professional duties. If the candidate can see that it is his or her "ox being gored" and his or her immediate work environment and climate being influenced, then he or she will provide significant insights into the matter. Do not try to avoid subjective and biased inputs. They are the stuff of informal process internalization, the habits that drive the way things are done every day of the week. Membership balance and the PIC itself will mitigate unfavorable tenancies of personal biases. And remember Shuster's law about people's inherent integrity. Lean on it. It works!

Expertise means that member candidates have significant knowledge, skill, insight, and experience about the topic to be investigated. It always helps to have people who know what they are talking about.

Control emphasizes having at least some members on the team who have the authority to do something about it,that is, who can implement final recommendations and gain the attention of those who can assist in enforcing implementation. These people become especially useful during causation and solution consequence analyses. It is a mistake to assume that they will be "nay sayers," always raising practical objections to innovative ideas. They often want things to change more than most other people.

Accessibility refers to gaining access to required data and information. Nothing is more frustrating to team members than to begin a PIC verification step without the foggiest idea about where pertinent data are to be found and how to obtain them. I usually advise people to seek one team member who has significant data-gathering and analysis experience. Someone who is talented with personal computers is also very useful. The ability to gather, manipulate, analyze, summarize, and present data saves all sorts of grief. Another accessibility talent involves knowing people and understanding the informal channels of communication that lead to meaningful information. These are the individuals who can usually say, "don't worry, I know who has it . . . I'll get it." I call these people *trackers*. Find one . . . at least one . . . for each team.

Availability means that every member, once selected, will be present at every meeting except under the most unusual and extreme circumstances. Nothing destroys a team faster than no-shows. Every possible negative "vibe" is communicated to team peers by continuous absences of one person or, even worse, periodic absences of a few people every session. You have seen how the PIC works. It must be obvious by now that consensus at every step is the single most important ingredient for advancing to the next step. And by definition, one cannot be satisficed by a set of team conclusions if one played no role in diverging/converging these conclusions. There are schemes for assigning alternate members, but that method of covering . . . and thereby legitimizing absences . . . is not satisfactory enough to discuss. I do not care how valuable a particular member would be with respect to the other criteria. If he or she cannot attend regularly, then what good is the absent value? Teams can always tap a person's special skills and knowledge in between-session interviews. What more can I say. *Be there!*

Commitment comes from everyone else in the organization. The clarion call of nay-sayers includes such statements as "nuts, things will never change around here," "yeah, it's a great idea, but now isn't the time. Let's wait until things clear up," "no way, we'll do all this and some supervisor will laugh at us and the managers will pat us on the back and ignore our results," and on . . . and on. These are honest feelings being expressed. They represent perceived history. Therefore, when a member's supervisor walks up to his or her desk and mutters "what again . . . another meeting? When is all this nonsense gonna end so you can get back to work? Just remember, you still have to get those reports out," their morale plummets. An even more insidious form of guilt-loading comes from within members themselves. If the outer support system dumps on them, their own sense of professional integrity will undermine their morale and motivation as they see their daily workload pile up on their desk. That is their integrity talking . . . their own sense of responsibility. It needs nurturing.

None of this has to happen. Environmental support can prevent it. Reread Chapter 3. This is what commitment is all about. In companies where top-level management commitment exists, this malady is minimized and can be effectively countered. But where only endorsement prevails, and the bottom-up path must be traveled, lack of commitment for **Teaming** efforts can demoralize people to a point of exhaustion. This is when the real quality improvement heroes emerge. They are the champions who eventually turn endorsement into commitment.

Therefore, when choosing team members, be sure that candidates are going to get the kind of environmental commitment they require to do the job.

When No EC/DT Matrix Exists

How do QATs get started when no EC/DT matrix exists? Where do topics for consideration originate? My answer to these questions should be obvious by now. The topics come from . . . individuals. They come from executive and management sponsors, who, as individuals, see a need and are willing and able to mobilize a team. Organizational muscle is required to release people, but there is usually enough endorsement drifting around to find members. Remember, the trick is to avoid trying to "convince the unconvincible." A willing and able mixture of people who satisfy (or satisfice) the six selection criteria can be found.

Do not be discouraged by the preceding paragraphs. It can be tough getting started, but so can getting up in the morning. All things considered, it is worth it. I do not want you approaching this effort wearing rose-tinted glasses, but neither do I want you to enter anticipating failure. Like hanging . . . it is only the first few minutes that hurt.

Team Leadership and Facilitating

Facilitators have one job during the meeting: to make **Teaming** as easy as possible. All else follows. A facilitator is teacher, coach, counselor, guide, encourager, watcher, listener, limiter, and all-around guru. Process and technique are his or her legitimate territory. But when it comes to influencing the substantive topic of team investigation, the guideline for the facilitator is "do not interfere." A facilitator ensures that the PIC and its techniques are properly exercised. But tampering with content is wrong. That is why facilitating is so difficult. It requires sensitivity in every aspect of human relations.

In matters of style, there are intrusive and extrusive facilitators. *Intrusive* facilitators are active. They do more direct guiding and leading of members through the process. *Extrusive* facilitators are passive. They do more listening and adjusting as members are guided through the process by their appointed or elected leader, who is also a member (and must then wear two hats). With new teams, I tend to be intrusive. This is a personal choice in style. Some of my colleagues disagree with me and are more extrusive. But we all agree that our only proper area of involvement is process/techniques. Those who interfere in content are simply "butinskies."

My feeling is that newcomers have enough to think about just learning the process and working on the issue. They can learn leadership and scribing (which I also do) later. I involve facilitator trainees in groups; first as observers, then as scribes, and then as facilitators on specific techniques. They learn best by doing, and team members are always supportive of peers who are willing and able to help them. This method also shows newcomers that they, too, can become expert on the process.

Doing It

As mentioned earlier, Chapters 5 and 6 discuss the formal elements of the PIC. But we all know that doing it involves human foibles and uncertainties. When in doubt, remember Shuster's Law #6: "The process will set you free!" As introduced early in Chapter 6, this guideline reminds us that the best way out of trouble is to recall where you are in the process and the technique and follow the rules. Sure as a tow truck, they will pull you out of the snowbank. Also remember that consensus rules, not leaders and facilitators. But that does not mean that a majority rules. Do not "go along to get along." Seek satisficing consensus, not total satisfaction. Remember that nothing is ever lost in the process. Items voted out as finalists in one step have an unerring tendency to crop up again in later steps. Nothing is irrevocable. And use common sense. It is no violation of convergence, for instance, if during lobbying, further clarification of a statement is requested. How can people evaluate what they cannot understand? Time after time, I have heard team members ask if further combining is allowed during multivoting. Why not? Just do it by the book. Obtain team consensus on reopening combining. If someone objects, then talk it out according to the rules of CDAM modifying; that is, encourage disputants to concentrate on areas of agreement rather than areas of disagreement. And let others suggest a consensus compromise.

Rarely, very rarely, I run into someone who is intent on "exposing this farce." It usually happens during orientation sessions. Smart facilitators leave people like that to other participants. They soon tire of such behavior. But the facilitator must not back down. Firm direction and insistence on process and techniques are vital. It is also necessary for the facilitator to talk to such individuals privately during breaks. It is vital that the individual participate, for example, say, at least, "pass" during divergence and remain quiet when appropriate. No one is obliged to suffer rudeness. What really settles the issue with such people is to ask them at the end of a Diverge/Converge exercise if the chosen finalists satisfice him or her. In my experience the answer has always been yes. They begin to reconsider at that point. A facilitator would be wrong to treat such individuals, at first glance, as troublemakers. Sometimes they are just supremely skeptical of any new fad that comes their way every year or two. Positive but firm approaches to these rare individuals are appropriate.

One thing that almost every team can expect is what I call "sophomore dip." It refers to a significant decline in team members' interest, motivation, attitudes, and performance that is not unlike a similar phenomenon that hits second-year college students. The initial excitement of it all has worn off and the reality of hard work hits home. There is only one cure for the dip. Give a few words of encouragement, admit the feeling and . . . press on. It is just like falling off a horse. Climb back on! You can tell newcomers to PIC that it is no panacea, that it requires diligence and hard work. But no one can foresee or control the attitudes and expectations that people bring into the room. So be prepared for it, let everyone know about it, and deal with it when it occurs. Some colleagues suggest that it not be mentioned, lest the warning create expectations and a self-fulfilling prophesy. I totally disagree. If I, as a facilitator, cannot explain things to people without engendering in them fears that, like Pygmalion, create the very situation to be feared, then perhaps I should seek a new profession. Also, it speaks ill of my respect for peoples' intelligence, if I assume that they cannot discern between limited conditional possibilities and certain prophesies. Remember, trust people and respect their dignity and intelligence.

One final word about atmosphere. Have fun! The PIC can be fun if we let it be so. The source of the pleasure and fun is the lack of both intimidation and the requirement to justify one's statements, the prohibition against negative statements and attacks on persons, and the fact that discussions are not permitted during the process. Some people suspect that it is logically inconsistent to claim that everyone can fully express themselves while, at the same time, discussions are strictly prohibited. But think about those meetings when agendas died under the onslaught of seemingly endless debates between two or more participants about any and all topics of choice. The key to individual freedom of expression is best assured by deriving a collective consensus to respect a like freedom for everyone. That idea is at least as old as social contract theory. And it is valid. Empower people through liberation.

Now that you have read it, "try it . . . you'll like it."

A SYSTEMS THEORY OF DECISION MAKING

Appendix II provides a detailed review of a theory that, I believe, explains why such participative decision-making devices as PIC work so well. It is based on the premise that the secret to organizational survival, like that of organic survival, is positive adaptation to environmental stress. Positive adaptation means more than simply bending with the wind. It means capturing the energy of a storm and using it to enhance one's own purposes.

The secret to positive adaptation is feedback, that is, reading the consequences of behavior and using that knowledge to adjust future actions. The study of such mechanisms became known as *systems analysis* several decades ago. Precise mathematical models of feedback systems developed in the engineering sciences as *control systems theory*. Every social science picked up on the trend after World War II, often referring to such studies as *input/output analysis*.

Basically, the idea is that a *system* is composed of any two or more interrelated things (objects, entities, events, and so on). The focus is less on the things, themselves, and more on the web of interrelatedness linking the things. Systems function by converting environmental *inputs* into planned *outputs*. Every system exists within an environment. Inputs are transactions from the environment into the system. Outputs are transactions from the system into the environment.

Very simply, a box-making machine is a system that takes cardboard, glue and tape from the environment, processes them, and converts them into a box. The box leaves the box-making system and reenters the environment. Electricity, hydraulic fluid, and lubricants are the energy and support inputs that sustain the system. The instructions and raw materials are the demand inputs that the system is to process and convert. The rate and character of the machine's acceptance of the raw materials depend on the character of the boxes. If all the boxes appear as specified, then acceptance of the demand items and instructions remains constant. But what if the instructions change to demand 20-cubic-foot square boxes instead of the earlier demanded 50-cubic-foot rectangular boxes? If the outputs do not change, then something must be altered, either within the system itself or in the input mixture . . . or both. For the system to adapt to this new stress, information to the effect that the output is now incorrect must be fed back to the input. And appropriate mechanisms must be installed to accept that information and act on it.

This principle is no less valid in a behavioral system. The simple act of inputting a rough manuscript into a memorandum-making system is predicated on the same notion. The output should be an appropriate memorandum. Sustenance (life-giving energy) comes from the support that people give to the process. Demand is represented by the rough manuscript and the procedure guidelines and instructions.

The value of this theory to our topic is that it explains why and how participative devices such as the PIC ensure that organizational systems stream-line and support the processing and conversion of legitimate demands into appropriate outputs, thereby reducing the effects of stress.

Quality improvement processes dilute stress by increasing an organization's ability to positively adapt to the threats inherent in a risky, uncertain, and competitive market environment. Consistent with a central thesis of this book, adaptive talents can be found only in individual human beings. The discussion in Appendix II details these linkages.

The Quality-Survival Ladder

The quality-survival ladder is a seven-rung steppingstone that summarizes the logical linkages between individuals and corporate survival. It is a direct outgrowth of the PIC/systems analysis synergy. Reading backward, from survival through the individual, it states that:

- ○ Survival . . . comes from . . . competitive position.
- ○ Competitive position . . . comes from . . . effectiveness.
- ○ Effectiveness . . . comes from . . . continuous performance improvement.
- ○ Continuous performance improvement . . . comes from . . . QI processes.
- ○ QI processes . . . come from . . . knowledge, skill, application.
- ○ Knowledge, skill, application . . . come from . . . commitment.
- ○ Commitment . . . comes from . . . individual character.

Note that the term productivity is absent from the ladder. Think of productivity as inherent in "competitive position." In other words, the traditional emphasis on productivity as an elemental feature of performance, that is, as an "act," is reversed. Productivity, in quality management, is the *result* of acts, of performance, just as is competitive position. Productivity, as *efficiency*, is a by-product of quality, as *effectiveness*. This represents the kind of radical departure in outlook that quality management requires in the journey from traditional management. No wonder it takes time. The traditional emphasis on quotas and getting things out surrenders to "doing the right thing, the right way, the first time." Acceptable quality levels are not inspected at the end of a process. Perfection is built in at the start. Standards of performance do not emanate from within the company, but rather from the customers who are served by the company. Manufacturers no longer create products. They serve customers. Doctors no longer treat illnesses. They treat people. Therefore, all suppliers are the same. Private or public, profit or not for profit, manufacturing or service, they all serve clients.

We are left with an axiom stressed by quality improvement specialists everywhere:

PRODUCTIVITY COMES FROM QUALITY . . .
QUALITY DOES NOT COME FROM PRODUCTIVITY.

This means that continued and prolonged stress on productivity will eventually erode both quality and productivity. But continued and prolonged stress on quality will improve both factors, thereby enhancing competitive position.

Parting Words

Thus, we come to the end of this essay. We have examined one corner of one aspect of quality management. But a very vital corner it is. And a very large aspect.

Remember, quality management is not wish fulfillment. No amount of schools and seminars will internalize the proper culture and performance. The wonderful ideas and motivation that popular sessions on quality improvement provide are well worth your time, energy, and expense. I heartily recommend them to one and all. But, eventually, their seemingly bottomless pit of ideas must be actualized. They must be redefined in operational terms in order to ultimately affect performance and induce appropriate changes. They require mechanisms to sustain continuous performance improvement, conformance to requirements, fitness for use, or whatever else you choose to call quality.

In actualizing terms, quality management can be defined as:

A MANAGEMENT *PHILOSOPHY*
THAT *INSPIRES* AND *COMMITS* EVERY *INDIVIDUAL*
TO VISIBLY AND ACTIVELY *PARTICIPATE*
IN THE DEVELOPMENT, NURTURING AND SUSTAINING
OF A WORKING *CULTURE*
THAT PURSUES THE *ETHIC*
OF TOTAL CUSTOMER SATISFACTION
THROUGH *DEDICATION* TO
CONTINUOUS PROCESS PERFORMANCE IMPROVEMENT

This book is about actualizing. It provides, I hope, an indepth look at one mechanism for turning ideas into action. And it shows you "what it takes." I do hope that it gives you . . . hope. This work is, indeed, a gospel . . . a call to arms and a tale of good news.

Teaming works!

APPENDIX

SHUSTER'S LAWS

APPENDIX

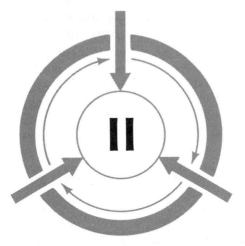

SYSTEM AND ENVIRONMENT

Organizations that are conducting serious inquiries into quality improvement seem to share a common fear, seldom voiced out loud prior to their inquiry. Their anxiety comes from the nagging worry that, against all accepted expectations, the company might not survive in an increasingly competitive environment. This raises the terrible spector of unemployment for all, setbacks in professional careers for many, and total loss of earning power for some. Little wonder that they are willing to consider radical changes in the very habits and culture that shape their corporate behavior. A quest for survival, then, is a common denominator for all organizations, public and private, manufacturing and service, profit and nonprofit.

What is it about innovative quality improvement processes that make them so successful as devices for increasing the chances of competitive survival? The answer is *positive adaptation*. Positive adaptation is the surest key to competitive survival.

To adapt means to bring an organism into correspondence with the reality of a situation, that is, to creatively adjust, reconcile, and fit. To be adaptable is to be pliable, supple, tractable, and moldable. To positively adapt means to proactively use reality for the direct benefit of the organism. Organizations displaying these qualities survive by finding ways to mobilize their human resources in support of their interests. Innovative quality improvement processes provide that proactive way. They direct and focus collective talents and energies to best exploit and capture individual creative potentials for adaptation, growth, and fulfillment.

Stress: Risk, Uncertainty, and Change

Competitive survival would hardly be a problem for anyone if the future was 100 percent predictable. However, our horizons are quite unpredictable, and our reach is but a guess. For each answer sought, for each question asked, for each alternative contemplated, there stands in our way the *risk* of failure, the *uncertainty* of outcome and the inevitability of *change*. Together these three potentially demoralizing agents inject *stress* into an organization's decision makers' hearts and minds. Positive adaptation allows them to overcome stress through preparation, attitude adjustment, and direct action. They need not passively endure stressful confrontations and merely hope to emerge from the fray with less than mortal wounds. They can purposefully turn stress around on itself and convert lurking dangers into welcome opportunities.

It is important, then, to understand the linkages through which positive adaptation allows individuals (acting collectively) to redirect and overcome stress. *Systems analysis* provides a useful model for clarifying those linkages, that is, for explaining how the PIC, for instance, promotes adaptation. The device gained wide popularity in both the physical and social sciences after World War II.

Systems Analysis

Systems Analysis does not focus on *things*. It pertains, rather, to *relationships between things*. Thus, a systems analyst in an automobile manufacturing plant would not concentrate on physical equipment, such as a clutch or transmission (things). He or she would, instead, be interested in how the two units work together (relate) to transmit mechanical energy from the engine to the wheels. The systems analyst thinks about the pattern of interactions and interdependencies that form a unified set of actions and behaviors joining the individual parts into an *integrated* whole.

This idea is not isolated to relationships between inanimate objects. It applies just as directly to relationships between people. It is applicable to this study because it provides useful insights into how organizations can mobilize human resources to adapt to stress.

A *system* is comprised of any two or more interrelated things. Thus a clutch and a transmission (two things) interrelate to transmit mechanical energy to a driveshaft. They are also part of the larger automobile system that performs to transport people and cargo. Similarly, individual people joining to act in a PIC team form a system designed to improve performance quality and productivity.

The simplest notion of an operating system is illustrated in Figure AII-1. Whatever kind of system is under consideration, it does not exist in a vacuum. It exists in the world; that is, the world is its *environment* (E). For instance, an automobile exists within the world, and the world is its environment ... within limits. Those limits circumscribe the areas of the world that will most probably be the car's immediate environment. The probability that a Chevy will be found 100 feet off of the ground suspended in an Amazon jungle tree is surely less than the probability of its sighting on the Los Angeles Santa Monica Freeway.

Systems are constantly interacting with their environment. Some interactions are stressful. For instance, a seashore climate will more than likely cause rust to corrode the body of a car. Conversely, the protective environment of a garage might shield the car from salt damage. Think of interactions as kinds of *transactions* between the environment and the system. There are two basic kinds of transactions: *inputs* (I) and *outputs* (O). Inputs are transactions moving from the environment into the system. Outputs move from the system into the environment. For instance, a human driver presses down on the accelerator of our Chevy, which represents an input communicating the command "move." The Corvette (we might as well enjoy our fantasy) system processes the command, culminating in the output of "wheels turning and car moving." In other words, a system can be thought of as a *processing* or *conversion* device. It *processes* inputs and *converts* them into outputs.

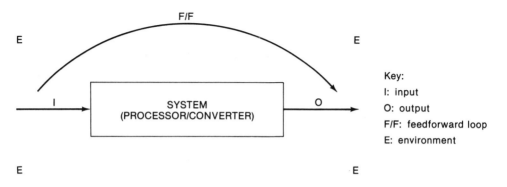

Figure AII-1 Simple Systems Model

Carrying the automobile analogy further, think of an internal combustion engine as a system. It converts chemical energy (air and gasoline) inputs into a mechanical energy (shaft torque) output. Similarly, a generator is a system that processes mechanical energy (shaft torque) and converts it into electrical energy (voltage and current) outputs. In the car, the engine and the generator perform as a system to charge the battery. The principle is no less applicable to a PIC team. The team processes input conditions and converts them into output, implementing actions. And we have already seen how important the setting or environment is to the health and success of any PIC group.

Transactions moving in the direction input–system–output are said to be moving in the *feedforward* (F/F) direction. Systems are designed to feedforward inputs into outputs.

The simplest kinds of systems described in Figure AII-1 are incomplete for our purposes. We are seeking a model that explains how systems positively adapt to stress and survive because of their adaptability.

Adapting systems are most simply illustrated in Figure AII- 2. Systems

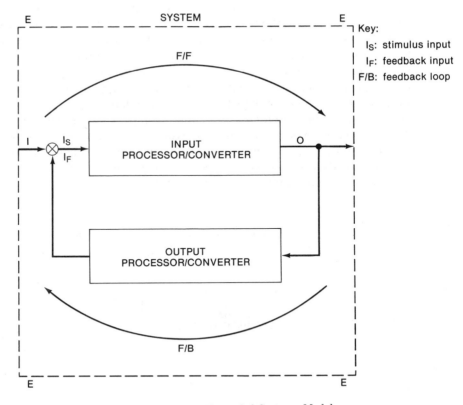

Figure AII-2 Expanded Systems Model

adapt through the mechanism of *feedback* (F/B). Note that the direction of feedback information is output–system–input, the reverse of feedforward. Feedback information communicates the character of the system's output response to an input, thereby allowing the initiator to appropriately adjust his or her requirement (and the input). For instance, assume that the Chevy's driver wants to accelerate from 40 to 60 mph. The speedometer and the driver comprise the system's *output converter*, because it is through them that the *feedback input* (I_F) is communicated to the input (accelerator). The driver desires 60 mph (I), 20 mph greater than (I_F). Therefore, the *stimulus input* (I_S) is $+20$ mph. The circled X symbol is employed in control systems theory to indicate the mixing of inputs into a combined resultant input (I_S). In this example, the mathematical summation is simple algebraic addition. In most behavioral systems, the precise character of the *summation network* is seldom reduceable to unequivocal and precise mathematical formulation.

Seeing the difference between the current and desired speeds, the driver presses the accelerator. That is the mechanism through which (I_S) is input into the system. Assume that the car accelerates to 55 mph. Then I remains 60 mph, but I_F is now 55 mph (assuming that the speedometer is accurate and the driver can read and interpret it). Now I_S is $+5$ mph. The pressure on the accelerator must now be eased, *adapting* to the fact that the current pressure, continued, will accelerate the vehicle beyond the desired speed of 60 mph. In other words, the driver is *adapting* to the actual changing conditions of vehicle acceleration and speed with respect to the desired speed (through feedback). The reader can imagine the changes in input parameters if the road becomes hilly and the system must respond to consequent speed variations. Cruise control systems replace the speedometer/driver as the output converter elements with a computer.

The output converter is the feedback loop processor/converter. It acts on the output (O) the same way that the feedforward loop input converter acts on the stimulus input (I_S). Assuming that the feedback loop is fault-free, then Feedback Input (I_F) should be an exact representation or *analog* of the output (O). For instance, in our car analogy, the actual output is the car accelerating to 60 mph. The output converter is comprised of the speedometer mechanism and driver (or a cruise control device). If the speedometer malfunctions or the driver is unable, for some reason, to see or interpret it, then the feedback input (I_F) will not correspond to the Output (O). Although the car's velocity reaches 60 mph, for instance, the speedometer might read 55 mph and the driver's perception of the car's speed will be incorrect. He or she will, therefore, continue to accelerate the auto until (I_F) equals 60 mph, at which time the car's actual speed (O) will be greater than the figure.

Extending this concept to the PIC, the reader should recognize this process operating throughout its techniques. The very essence of the PIC is to apply individual creativity and collective consensus making to corporate stresses, in the interest of deriving feasible working adaptation resolutions.

The complexity of large organizations sometimes muddies the waters of adaptation analysis, regardless of the model being employed. It might be trite to repeat the old saying that human behavior is complex, but it is also true. And it is against this background that the real value of the systems model, as a device for clarifying adaptive processes, is illuminated. Figure AII-3 includes input elements in the model that add the perspective needed to cut through some of the complexities of human behavior analysis. The central themes of these additions were introduced by political scientists such as David Easton, from the University of Chicago, in the early 1950s. They were interested in a question very similar to ours: "What is it that makes political systems survive under stress?"

System Inputs

In the refined model illustrated in Figure AII-3, the input (I) is seen to be a summation of two major tributaries. The first tributary is *demands* (D). The second is *sustenance* (S) or life support. Recall that every system is designed to fulfill the purposes of its customers. The Chevy system, for instance, is designed to fulfill the transportation requirements of its users. Demands are inputs reflecting the wants of users. When the driver of the car presses the accelerator, shifts the gears, presses the brakes or turns the wheel, he or she is initiating a *demand* into the car system from which he or she expects corresponding outputs.

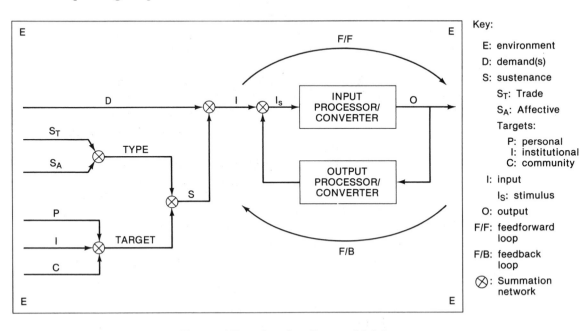

Figure AII-3 Complete Systems Model

This principle is no less active in organizations. Individuals and departments are literally bombarded with demands for some new piece of information, immediate action, expanded responsibility, revised documentation, faster service, or other infinitely various outputs over time. In a perfect organization, one might expect that all inputs would represent demands consistent with corporate goals and that the output responses would exactly correspond to and satisfy those demands. But how familiar are the cries heard about personal conflicts, interdepartment conflicts, territoriality, special interests, hidden agendas, poor attitudes, indifference, split loyalties, and a basket of other negative factors that demoralize people and cripple performance. These stress forces act quite independently of the demand-process/convert-output function. A question can be legitimately asked about the extent to which human responses in organizations are more a function of the above cited debilitating forces and less a function of pure legitimate demands. The systems model suggests that the input (I) is, indeed, a mixture of demands and other factors, combined in Figure AII-3 as input (S), *sustenance.*

Sustenance means life support, that is, the energy that enables the system to function. In the car engine, sustenance is provided by air and gasoline. Without these two fuels, the engine could not come to life and function to process inputs into outputs. Even with air and gasoline, the performance of the engine, that is, its ability to accelerate on demand or run smoothly, depends on the character of the air and the gasoline. At high altitudes, for instance, the air might be too thin to sustain expected engine performance. Perhaps the octane rating of the gasoline is less than adequate for the engine's design parameters. If so, then the engine will knock and performance will degrade. Consequently, when the demand "accelerate" is input, it will be mixed with the sustenance input "thin air" or "low octane gasoline," and the delivered output, "increased speed," will be degraded in response to the composite input.

The status of the engine, itself, can affect sustenance. If the air and gasoline are both satisfactory, for instance, but the engine is out of tune or the carburetor is clogged, then overall engine life support will diminish. Therefore, if sustaining fuels are absent or if the system is incapable of incorporating available sustenance, its ability to properly accept, process, and convert demands into appropriate outputs will be degraded or eliminated.

People provide the inputs to human organization systems. The members of the system, employees, perform the bulk of processing/converting in both the feedforward and feedback loops. They also place substantial demands on the organization. But it is the sustenance input that they inject into the system that can be viewed as the key factor determining the health of the corporation, that is, its ability to effectively process and convert in both loops. Vendors (resource suppliers) and customers (output users and sponsors) also have significant roles to play in this process, but the focus here is on the employees as contributors and receivers of stress ... *all* employees ... at *every* level of responsibility.

Consider all the familiar conflicts and special interests that impose corrosive stress on organizations. This model is supposed to clarify the mechanism of corrosion and show why quality improvement processes, including the PIC, reverse the sickness and rehabilitate the patient. A complete examination of the sustenance input in Figure AII-3 and Table AII-1 provides the necessary clues to answer these issues.

Consider the sustenance (S) input and all its subsidiary elements as a composite of all the life support attitudes and behaviors inputting from each employee and the many subcultures and coalitions that form among pockets of individuals. Broken down into its parts, this composite S would be replaced in the figure with a dense crowd of S inputs feeding into the I summation network.

The life support that human beings give to an organization is not chemical, as was the sustenance offered by air and gasoline to the engine. It comes, rather, from behavior. An individual need not be enthusiastic, happy, content, excited, or devoted to a group to sustain it. He need only act in a manner that, ultimately, supports general progress toward corporate goals. Sometimes the most disenchanted of us plod through the years, miserable or indifferent, all the while contributing part of our skills (that minimal amount necessary to meet some set requirement). To the extent that individual performance is less than would occur with fully motivated incentives, stress has eroded the character, quantity, and content of desired outputs.

All the complex and various forces, then, that combine to stress an organization can be thought of as culminating in the system input of sustenance (S). Sustenance can therefore provide a measure of the level of stress active in a system. Once measured, actions can be taken to reduce or eliminate the causes, thereby increasing the organization's ability to adapt and survive.

Working backward from S, in Figure AII-3, overall sustenance is shown to be a summation to two *types*, *trade* sustenance and *affective* sustenance. Remember that individual human behavior is the mechanism through which life-sustaining energy is transmitted to the organization. Therefore, sustenance flows from the individual to the group. *Trade sustenance* is contractual in nature and involves little or no emotional or linking features. It involves quid pro quo standards, that is, this for that, something for something, one for one. For instance, an employee might work overtime for many reasons, one of which is that he is promised extra pay or compensatory time off. This person might entertain only the very slightest interest in the work or its outcome, but he works the overtime to receive an explicitly agreed on return. The employee's behavior, therefore, sustains the organization. Note that the system output was as much determined by its ability to process/convert the S input factor (work only for explicit return) as it was by its ability to process/convert the D input. The two inputs were quite independent, and in the purest analytical sense the worker's decision to contribute was not influenced by D.

The second type of life support is *affective sustenance*. By far the most important of the two types for stress reduction, its origin is in the emotional linkages that bind an individual to the organization. Terms such as loyalty, devotion, belonging, patriotism, satisfaction, happiness, and attachment are modifiers and descriptors that come to mind when the subject is broached. Were this type of sustenance flowing from the worker toward the organization, then the overtime would be performed with little or no regard for an explicit return. The binding affection linking the person to the group would guarantee a level of involved performance not contemplated in the earlier case.

The principle conclusion to be drawn from this characterization of the types of sustenance is that:

ORGANIZATIONS CANNOT ADAPT SUFFICIENTLY TO SURVIVE IN A COMPETITIVE ENVIRONMENT IF THE SUSTENANCE OFFERED BY ITS EMPLOYEES IS PRIMARILY TRADE SUSTENANCE.

Consider the dilemma of the supervisor requesting that one, and only one, of three employees work the overtime, assuming that the three tend to be largely trade sustenance oriented. Assume that two of the workers have been requesting overtime (exclusively for the extra income) and that the third person consistently expresses distaste for overtime. There is hardly a satisfactory alternative choice that the supervisor can make. At least one person will be dissatisfied with each overtime selection alternative, and that person's sustenance will diminish all the more, adding to an already overburdened atmosphere of stress. If one of the two who desire extra income is selected, then no retentive sustenance grows from his or her quarter. He simply trades something for something and no affective linkages have been bonded to lessen future stress.

Worse yet, the no-overtime worker might have to be selected, in which case the tiny quid pro quo of money for overtime will be overwhelmed by negative feelings (and consequent further erosion of scarce affective sustenance) engendered in all three of the individuals. The fact is that in organizations where affective sustenance is minimal almost every decision will tend to erode it further, because in the very act of meeting the needs of one employee, a manager is likely to deny a need to one or more of the other individuals.

However, had the atmosphere been one of high affective sustenance, the overtime selection would have involved little or no stress factors. People imbued with positive feelings about the organization and their place and worth within it can absorb unwelcome decisions as necessary and functional. They can even reinforce their positive overall orientation toward the organization through the satisfaction of sacrificing a personal interest for the good of all. The principle to be drawn from this characterization of the types of sustenance is that:

ORGANIZATIONS CAN ADAPT SUFFICIENTLY TO SURVIVE IN A
COMPETITIVE ENVIRONMENT IF THE SUSTENANCE OFFERED BY
ITS EMPLOYEES IS PRIMARILY AFFECTIVE SUSTENANCE.

The two principles of sustenance, are illustrated in the forth column of
Table AII-1, Positive Impact on Stress Erosion. For the trade type, the impact
is low (or even negative). For the affective type, the impact is high. Therefore,
one crucial assessment to be made within an organization is the prevailing
pattern of sustenance by type. From this single parameter, much can be
inferred and correctives estimated.

The other vital parameter of sustenance is its *target*, that is, the object(s)
toward which it is aimed and directed (targeted). Returning to the overtime
example, assume that the disenchanted employee displaying only trade sustenance targets his or her very negative affective orientation toward one person,
Joe Smith, the immediate supervisor. In fact, his or her feelings about the organizational structure, policies, and general procedures are not really so negative. But the person in the supervisory position immediately over him or her
poisons the working environment enough to blacken his or her overall mood
and contribution. The employee's target might not be the immediate supervisor, but a manager several steps removed, or more than one manager, or even
one or more working peers. The point is that the targets of discontent are individuals . . . specific people. This focus of sustenance toward human individuals
(positive or negative) is called the *personal target* (P).

If sustenance targeted at the personal level is negative, then the stress it
causes can be relieved by a shift in personnel assignments or by accommodations between the individuals involved. Rotations occurring in the normal
course of time can often relieve the pressures debilitating personal sustenance
and its consequent stress. Sometimes the positive attitudes aimed toward the
other two sustenance targets are enough to mitigate the impact of their nega-

TABLE AII-1 Impact of Sustenance on System Performance

Sustenance Type	Sustenance Target			Positive Impact on Stress Erosion
	P	I	C	
Trade	1	2	3	Low
Affective	4	5	6	High
	Low	→	High	
Positive Impact on Stress Erosion				

tive counterparts targeted at P. As stressful as P-targeted negative sustenance can be in an organization, its impact will be less threatening to the overall corporate body than a like occurrence at the other two targets.

The second target of sustenance is institutions (I). Its focus is the organizational structure (roles, policies, procedures, rules, offices, charters, and established patterns of interaction) defining how and where people are to associate within the corporate system boundary. Lack of I-targeted positive sustenance is potentially far more stressful than lack of P-targeted support. The target this time is not a person, but a regulated and imposed element of the authority structure. It is no longer true that the worker is unhappy with Joe Smith. He might be delighted with Joe. But the very position of supervisor that Joe currently occupies (the role) is the target of the worker's dismay, along with all the organizational arrangements subsumed within that department. Indeed, the worker's discomfort might extend to wider corporate horizons, for example, the total organization chart, policies, and procedures. If his or her low esteem for these institutions is shared across a sufficiently wide spectrum of people, a quiet but pervasive cloud of stress can drift over the assembly, intruding wisps of performance erosion that are, at once, difficult to perceive, evasive to grasp, impervious to admission of culpability by those whose interests it protects, and resistant to accommodation.

Stress introduced through negative I-directed sustenance cannot be eliminated so easily through interpersonal accommodations. This is what Deming (1982) means when he says that good workers cannot perform satisfactorily within an inherently poor system. The institutional arrangements are created and maintained by managers as the arena within which workers must function. Widespread I-targeted negative sustenance must be sensed as a legitimate input to the system, and it must be responded to through the system loops. Quality improvement processes are specially useful in improving I-targeted negative sustenance, if only because they encourage *networking* and because the issues they tend to illuminate bear directly on heretofore taboo issues of entrenched interests and associations of territory. Therefore, since I-targeted issues reach more deeply into the bowels of an organization than do P-targeted issues, it follows that successful reduction of negative I-targeted sustenance will have a greater and more fundamental positive impact on overall corporate stress than will reduction of its P-targeted counterpart.

Community-targeted sustenance (C) reaches into the very heart of an organization's reason for being. It gets to the issue of the worth of the enterprise itself. An extreme example of C-targeted negative sustenance would be reflected in a worker's deep concerns about his employer's chemical plant that seriously poisons the environment, or the weapons facility that manufactures death and destruction, or the publishing firm that distributes pornography and/or slanderous yellow journalism. These are, of course, *very* extreme examples. But they make the point. It is not unusual for people to find themselves caught in employment (from which they have no reasonable or probable hope of escape) that they find meaningless at best and rotten at worst. Their frustration is not directed toward individual people (P). Neither is it aimed at institutions or organizations (I). More fundamentally, it is targeted at the very taproots of the enterprise and can be cured by nothing less than the worker leaving the company, a reorientation of the worker's basic values, or a complete redirection of the corporate strategic mission and goals. Stress at this level can be truly fatal to any organization whose personnel suffer significant C-targeted negative sustenance. They are saying, in effect, that "our enterprise should not exist . . . or, at least, I should not be part of it!"

In summary, C-targeted positive sustenance is created in the act of one's joining an organization. The person is accepting a role in the corporate enterprise and is thereby absorbing some part of its activity and accountability.

The hierarchy of *positive impact on stress erosion* of the sustenance target is shown across the bottom of Table AII-1. The impact is lowest for P-targeted and highest for C-targeted sustenance. Reversing the perspective, it is obvious that the same low–high relationships hold for potential *negative impact on stress accumulation* of support targets. As shown, C-targeted negative sustenance is significantly more stressful and threatening to an organization's survival prospect than is its P-targeted counterpart.

The six cells of Table AII-1 are numbered 1 through 6. Category 1 represents *trade*-type/P-targeted (S_T/P) sustenance. Therefore, it is based on a *contractual*-type, "something-for-something" agreement between parties and carries little or no potential for binding emotional commitments. It is therefore the category with the least potential for affecting stress positively or negatively. The potential for having such impact increases with the cell (category) numbers. Category 6 has the greatest potential for stress impact because it is *affective*-Type/C-targeted (S_A/C), for all of the reasons given earlier.

One of the first things to assess in a quality-interested organization is its internal status with respect to the categories of sustenance defined in Table AII-1. This is a direct indicator of the levels and insidiousness of stress pervading the corporate culture. It is therefore a guidepost, illuminating the way toward stress alleviation, increasing adaptation capability, and increasing survival potential.

Implications

Systems analysis suggests that people respond to requests for reasons that might have little to do with the substance of the need (demand) requiring action. They might, instead, respond to perceived threats to interests deemed important to personal survival and position (sustenance). Do individuals, then:

Survive . . . to act in behalf of the organization? or
Act in behalf of the organization . . . to survive?

These are not unlike the questions raised in election studies; do elected officials run for election in order to serve the people or serve the people in order to be elected? Which of the two alternatives is the end and which the means? It should be understood that there is nothing inherently evil about acting in one's own interest. The intent here is to *understand* motives, not to *judge* them, to *fix* defects instead of blame.

The foregoing analysis implies that in organizations that suffer high degrees of internal stress, and where S_T dominates S_A, the latter ends–means motive is probable. The focus is less on customer needs and promoting corporate goals then it is on status maintenance. Such conditions are harbingers of limited adaptability to environmental changes and stresses and can be, ultimately, foretellers of corporate demise. But with a reversal of such internal stress conditions, the former alternative is likely. The focus shifts to the customer and promotion of the corporate mission. Such reversals do not just happen. They occur as the result of painstaking, positive, and continuous efforts to accumulate large deposits of S_A as bulwarks against the external stresses so sure to occur in the uncertain and risky competitive environment. They occur because heretofore blocked and broken F/F and F/B decision loops are rebuilt and opened, allowing the vital fluids of ideas and consensus to nurture the corporate body back to health.

A sense of continuity emerges from this growth, a confidence that one positive act will be followed by another. A perception of integration of interests slowly emerges (S_A) as problems earlier found to be intractable and chronic dissolve in ever widening circles (clearing loop channels). People begin to perceive just how dependent others really are on their performance (that what they do matters after all) and, logically, how they too depend on others. This sense of mutual interdependence of interests and performance grows slowly at first, but at an accelerating rate *if and only if* it is continuously fed.

The impetus needed to ensure continuous feeding comes from processes such as innovative quality improvement initiatives. As a part of such movements, the PIC inspires every positive element illuminated through systems analysis. Its capacity, for instance, to unlock and unclog F/F and F/B loops is enormous, but not more so than its ability to integrate personal interests and generate large accounts of S_A. Drawing its participating members from disparate divisions throughout an organization, individuals suddenly find themselves ensconced in a high-priority action enterprise with people whom they have likely never met and whom they have probably railed against as the ghostly "theys" that are constantly "fouling up" the works.

The eye-openings that criss-cross the PIC environment produce a shared, enlarged perspective and encourage each individual's natural tendency to confer on their new-found peers a sense of professional dignity impossible to imagine in prior settings. More than any other factor in quality improvement processes, this "people" element is the most important. This in no way minimizes the great value of techniques, measurement, and promotion, which are also central to such enterprises. But, in the last analysis, *people act* (Shuster's Law #1), and final accountability must attach to individuals, not to tools and devices.

The Quality-Survival Ladder

The systems model shows that adaptation to stress is the key to corporate survival in a competitive environment. The factors creating adaptability were illuminated and shown to be inherent elements of innovative quality improvement processes, including the PIC. With this established, a ladder of seven logically connected steps linking individuals directly to overall corporate survival can be constructed, which views organizations as dependent on its individual employees . . . *not* on its departments, divisions, other working groups, and formal structures. This difference in viewpoint is not merely semantic, it is not a play on words. Rather, the perceived split between individuals versus organization structures, as vital determinants of corporate strength, creates fundamentally different attitudes and behaviors. This is not a new idea. Alexander Hamilton called it the *fundamental* flaw of the Articles of Confederation and the *central* virtue of the proposed Constitution of 1787.

> The great and radical vice in the construction of the existing Confederation is in the principle of LEGISLATION for STATES or GOVERNMENTS, in their CORPORATE or COLLECTIVE CAPACITIES, and as contradistinguished from the INDIVIDUALS of whom they consist. Though this principle does not run through all the powers delegated to the Union, yet it pervades and governs those on which the efficacy of the rest depends . . . we must resolve to incorporate into our plan those ingredients which may be considered as forming the characteristic difference between a league and a government; we must extend the authority of the Union to the *persons of the citizens—the only proper objects of government.* (1788)

Advance the clock 200 years and shift your focus from effective governance of a political community to effective governance of a business organization, and the principle slips not a notch. It is universal for any collection of people intent on constructing a collective that is, at once, secure for the public and nurturing to the individual.

Working backward down the ladder from survival to people, the seven steps interact as follows:

1. Survival . . . comes from . . . competitive position.
2. Competitive position . . . comes from . . . effectiveness.
3. Effectiveness . . . comes from . . . continuous performance improvement.
4. Continuous performance improvement . . . comes from . . . QI processes.
5. QI processes . . . come from . . . knowledge, skill, application.

6. Knowledge, skill, application . . . come from . . . commitment.

7. Commitment . . . comes from . . . individual character.

The intermediate milestones of the ladder are familiar, having been discussed in Part I, as integral elements of the PIC. The ladder is a culmination of quality improvement and PIC principles.

Effective positive adaptation implies the capability of producing a desired result. This does not suggest that everyone *does*, always, produce a desired result. It only means that they possess a potential to do so. The character of an organization's *competitive position* is, therefore, dependent on the degree to which it acts on its potential. Acting on potential is the key to effectiveness and derives, as this appendix suggests, from the continuous application of *QI processes*, which have been shown to possess those highest virtues of systems that maximize the ability to adapt to stressful environmental conditions. The terms *knowledge, skill, and application*, together, mean that it is not enough to simply possess these virtues. It is necessary that they be applied, that is, *used* in a determined way within the context of quality improvement. Where does that determination come from? It can only come from one trait . . . *commitment*!

As discussed in Chapter 3, *commitment* means single-minded, obsessive intolerance for anything less than quality. Committed people will do whatever it takes to continuously improve and will settle only for perfection, with respect to that obligation. To be committed is an ethical choice that each individual must make within his or her own mind and heart.

We come full circle at this point. The PIC emphasizes that quality, at bottom, is a personal commitment; it is a *human* characteristic residing in the deepest values shaping each employee's sense of professional integrity. It is, at heart, an ethical prescription. This same theme was stressed in the systems model. Demands come from people. Sustenance, positive and negative, is felt (and targeted) by people. Feedback and feedforward loops are created, maintained, or destroyed by *people*. Outputs are generated by *people*. Thus, the Quality-Survival Ladder leans on personal values and integrity. And, in the end, the services that emanate from that level of quality performance so cherished in this and similar essays are motivated, initiated, and delivered for the benefit of *people*.

BIBLIOGRAPHY

SELECTED REFERENCES

BOOKS

DEUTSCH, KARL, *The Nerves of Government* (London: The Free Press of Glencoe, 1963).

DOWNS, ANTHONY, *An Economic Theory of Democracy* (New York: Harper & Row, 1957).

DRUCKER, PETER, *The Effective Executive* (New York: Harper & Row, 1967).

DUNCAN, W. JACK, *Decision Making and Social Issues* (Hinsdale, Ill.: Dryden Press, 1973).

EASTON, DAVID, *A Systems Analysis of Political Life* (New York: John Wiley & Sons, Inc., 1965).

ETZIONI, AMITAI, ed., *A Sociological Reader on Complex Organizations* (New York: Holt, Rinehart and Winston, 2nd. ed., 1969).

KEPNER, CHARLES, and BENJAMIN S. TREGOE, *The Rational Manager* (New York: McGraw-Hill, 1963).

MARCH, JAMES G., and HERBERT A. SIMON, *Organizations* (New York: Wiley, 1958).

MCGREGOR, DOUGLAS, *The Human Side of Enterprise* (New York: McGraw-Hill, 1963).

PARSONS, TALCOTT, and EDWARD A. SHILS, eds., *Toward A General Theory of Action* (New York: Harper & Row, 1951).

ROSSITER, CLINTON, *The Federalist Papers* (New York: The New Amercian Library, 1961).

SEILER, JOHN A., ed., *Systems Analysis in Organizational Behavior* (Homewood, Ill.: Richard D. Irwin and Dorsey Press, 1967).

SHERIF, MUZAFER, et al., *Intergroup Conflict and Cooperation: The Robbers Cave Experiment* (Norman, Okla.: University Book Exchange, 1961).

SMITH, ADAM, *Wealth of Nations* (New York: Modern Library, 1937).

STUBBERUD, ALLEN R., JOSEPH J. DISTEFANO, III, and IVAN J. WILLIAMS, *Theory and Problems of Feedback and Control Systems* (New York: McGraw-Hill Book Co., Schaum's Outline Series, 1967).

THIBAUT, JOHN W., and HAROLD H. KELLY, *The Social Psychology of Groups* (New York: Wiley, 1959).

YOUNG, STANLEY, *Management: A Systems Analysis* (Glenview, Ill.: Scott Foresman, 1968).

ARTICLES

BOULDING, KENNETH E., "The Ethics of Rational Decision," *Management Science*, 12, February, 1966 B-161–B-189.

BOWER, JOSEPH L., "The Role of Conflict in Economic Decision-Making Groups: Some Empirical Results," *Quarterly Journal of Economics*, May, 1965, 263–277.

CONTANT, MICHAEL, "Systems Analysis in the Appellate Decision-Making Process," *Rutgers Law Review*, 24, 1970, 293–322.

CRUTCHFIELD, RICHARD S., "Conformity and Character," *American Psychologist*, 10, 1955, 191–198.

ERICKSON, RICHARD F. "The Impact of Cybernetic Information Technology on Management Value Systems," *Management Science*, October, 1969, B-40–B-60.

FAUST, W. L., "Group Versus Individual Problem-Solving," *Journal of Abnormal and Social Psychology*, 59, 1959, 68–72.

GUETZKOW, HAROLD, and JOHN GYR, "An Analysis of Conflict in Decision-Making Groups," *Human Relations*, 7, 1954, 367–382.

HUBER, GEORGE P., and ANDRE DELBECQ, "Guidelines for Combining the Judgments of Individual Members in Decision Conferences," *Academy of Management Journal*, 15, June, 1972, 161–174.

LEWIN, KURT, "Frontiers in Group Dynamics," *Human Relations*, 1, 1947, 5–41, 141–153.

MASLOW, A. H. "A Theory of Human Motivation," *Psychological Review*, 50, 1943, 370–396.

SHUSTER, H. DAVID, "Greek and Medieval Thought and a Modern Problem of Social Obedience," *Unpublished paper presented to University of Rochester*, 1969.

SIMON, HERBERT A., "Administrative Decision Making," *Public Administration Review*, March, 1965, 31–37.

—————————, "A Behavioral Model of Rational Choice," *Quarterly Journal of Economics*, February 1955, 99–118.

WIEST, W. M., L. W. PORTER, and E. E. GHISELLI, "Relationship Between Individual Proficiency and Team Performance and Efficiency," *Journal of Applied Psychology*, 45, 1961, 435–440.

ADDITIONAL BOOKS

CORNFORD, FRANCIS M. (tr.), *The Republic of Plato* (New York: Oxford University Press, 1963).

JOWETT, B. (tr.), *The Dialogues of Plato*, Vols II & IV (New York: Random House, 1953).

RIKER, WILLIAM, H., *The Theory of Political Coalitions* (New Haven: Yale University Press, 1962).

SABINE, GEORGE H., *A History of Political Theory* (New York: Holt, Rinehart & Winston, 1962).

QUALITY IMPROVEMENT REFERENCES

ANDERSON, DOUGLAS N., *The Quality Evolution* (3M: Unpublished).

BARRA, RALPH, *"Putting Quality Circles to Work:* (New York: McGraw-Hill Book Co., 1983).

BETKER, HARRY A., *"Storyboarding: It's No Mickey Mouse Technique,"* Juran Report (Wilton, Ct: The Juran Institute, No. 5 Summer 1985), pp. 25–30.

BOTHE, DAVIS R., "Quantifying the Defects," *Quality* (Wheaton, Ill: Hitchock Publishing Co., Vol. 25, Feb. 1986), pp. 71–72.

CROCKER, OLGA L., SYRIL CHARNEY and JOHNNY SIK LEUNG CHIU, *Quality Circles: A Guide to Participation and Productivity* (New York: New American Library, 1984).

CROSBY, PHILIP B., *Quality Is Free* (New York: McGraw-Hill Book Co., 1979).

"Customer Order Quality," *Quality* (Wheaton, Ill: Hitchcock Publishing).

DEMING, W. E., *Quality, Productivity and Competitive Position* (MIT: Center for Advanced Engineering Study, 1982).

DMYTROW, ERIC D., "Process Capability in the Service Sector," *The Juran Report* (Wilton, CT: The Juran Institute, No. 5, Summer 1985), pp. 31–37.

FEIGENBAUM, ARMAN V., "Quality: The Strategic Business Imperative," *Quality Progress* (Milwaukee, WS: American Society for Quality Control, Inc., Feb. 1986), pp. 27–30.

——————————, "Total Quality Leadership," *Quality* (Wheaton, Ill: Hitchcock Publishing Co., Vol. 25, April 1986), pp. 18–22.

FINE, CHARLES H. and DAVID H. BRIDGE, *Managing Quality Improvement* (MIT: Unpublished, 1985).

GARVIN, DAVID A., *What Does "Product Quality" Really Mean* (Harvard University: Unpublished).

GRENIER, ROBERT, "Total Quality Assurance, Part IV," *Quality* (Wheaton, Ill: Hitchcock Publishing Co., Vol. 25, Feb. 1986), pp. 54–56.

——————————, "Total Quality Assurance, Part V," *Quality* (Wheaton, Ill.: Hitchcock Publishing Co., Vol. 25, April 1986), pp. 38–41.

HALPIN, JAMES, F., *Zero Defects* (New York: McGraw-Hill Book Co., 1966).

HOLMES, DONALD S. and A. ERHAN MERGEN, "Chi-Square vs. X & R Chart," *Quality* (Wheaton, Ill: Hitchcock Publishing Co., Vol. 25, Feb. 1986), pp. 60–61.

HOOGSTOEL, ROBERT E., "A Life Cycle for Quality Circles?" *The Juran Report* (Wilton, CT: The Juran Institute, No. 5, Summer 1985), pp. 23–24.

ISHIKAWA, KAURO, *Guide to Quality Control* (Tokyo: Asian Productivity Organization, 1976).

JURAN, JOSEPH, *Managerial Breakthrough* (New York: McGraw-Hill Book Co.), 1964.

_____, "Product Quality: A Prescription for the West," *Management Review* (New York: American Management Association, June/July 1981), Reprint.

_____, *Quality Control Handbook* (New York: McGraw-Hill Book Co., 1979).

_____, *Quality Planning & Analysis* (New York: McGraw-Hill Book Co., 1980).

KARABATSOS, NANCY A., "World Class Quality," *Quality* (Wheaton, Ill: Hitchcock Publishing Co., Vol. 25, Jan. 1986), pp. 14–18.

KEPNER, CHARLES H. and BENJAMIN B. TREGOE, *The New Rational Manager* (Princeton, NJ, Princeton Research Press, 1981).

LAFORD, RICHARD, "Don't Settle for More Inspectors," *Quality* (Wheaton, Ill: Hitchcock Publishing Co., Vol. 25, Jan. 1986, p. 46).

LIEBMAN, MURRAY E., "New Global Competitors," *Quality Progress* (Milwaukee, WS: American Society for Quality Control, Inc., Feb. 1986), pp. 58–60.

"Making Quality a Part of the Woodwork," *Quality* (Wheaton, Ill: Hitchcock Publishing Co., Vol. 25, March 1986), pp. 58–60.

MCDONALD, JAMES F., "Global Quality Manufacturing Strategy," *Quality Progress* (Milwaukee, WS: American Society for Quality Control, Inc., Feb. 1986), pp. 36–38.

MCGRATH, JAMES, "The Common Threads of Quality Improvement," *Quality* (Wheaton, Ill: Hitchcock Publishing Co., Oct. 1985).

O'BRIEN, WALTER J., "The Customer: A Global Profile," *Quality Progress* (Milwaukee, WS: American Society for Quality Control, Inc., Feb. 1986), pp. 24–25.

OLSEN, JANES E., "The Quality Challenge," *Quality Progress* (Milwaukee, WS: American Society for Quality Control, Inc., Feb. 1986), pp. 12–14.

PETERS, TOM and NANCY AUSTIN, *A Passion for Excellence: The Leadership Difference* (New York: Random House, Inc., 1985).

_____, and ROBERT H. WATERMAN, JR., *In Search of Excellence: Lessons from America's Best-Run Companies* (New York: Warner Books, Inc., 1982).

SULLIVAN, L.P., "Japanese Quality Thinking at Ford," *Quality Progress* (Wheaton, Ill: Hitchcock Publishing Co., Vol 25, April, 1986), pp. 32–34.

TAGUCHI GENICHI, *Introduction to Quality Engineering: Designing Quality into Products and Processes* (White Plains, New York: Kraus International Publications, 1986).

INDEX